Healing Emotional Wounds

Healing Emotional Wounds

David G. Benner

BAKER BOOK HOUSE
Grand Rapids, Michigan 49516

Copyright 1990 by
Baker Book House Company

ISBN: 0-8010-0983-9

Second printing, January 1993

Printed in the United States of America

Library of Congress Cataloging-in-Publication Data

Benner, David G.
    Healing emotional wounds / David G. Benner
        p.   cm.
    Includes bibliographical references.
    ISBN 0-8010-0983-9
    1. Emotions. 2. Suffering. 3. Adjustment (Psychology)
    I. Title.
    BF561.B42   1990
    152.4—dc20

                                                    90-35633
                                                    CIP

To my parents,
Gordon and **Margaret Benner**

Contents

Introduction
Invisible but Real

It wasn't that he was feeling sorry for himself. He simply wished that other people could better understand how he felt. "If only my leg was broken, or perhaps if I had cancer. Then they would know I was suffering. But no one sees me suffer. No one understands because no one sees my wound."

The invisible wound which this young man was carrying was an emotional one. He had experienced many years of belittling at the hands of an alcoholic and often cruel father, and the result was much inner emotional pain. In spite of putting on a good front with others, he was shy and lacking in self-confidence. Furthermore, he was often overwhelmed by bouts of depression and, alternating with these, waves of deep rage at his father. "Why can't I just leave all this behind me? Why must it continue to plague me? It was all so long ago!"

Like so many of us, this man carried in his person scars from past emotional hurts. These scars, as well as the underlying damage, are invisible to most of those around us. But we feel their effect, pain that is often at least as intense as that associated with any physical wound. We may at times feel confused by the nature of

9

these invisible wounds, wondering how things in the past can have such a continuing influence on us in the present. We may feel that because these hurts are not physical, they are somehow less real. Because of this we may even feel guilt over the continuing effects of the hurts. And in the event that we don't naturally respond with guilt, there will always be plenty of other people who help us feel guilty by telling us that we should be over the past hurts by now, that it is time to forget the past and to get on with life.

But sometimes this seems impossible. In spite of our best efforts to forget the hurts of the past, we continue to be in bondage to the memories and feelings associated with them. Or we may begin to get some distance from the emotions but our behavior betrays the continuing influence of the past hurt. Perhaps we are more withdrawn and emotionally isolated, or maybe less trusting. Or possibly we notice that we avoid certain situations associated with the past hurt, overreact to others, or seem to carry a chip on our shoulders. In all these ways we show that the hurt has not yet been healed. And until it is, we remain victims of it, bound to its tyrannizing effects.

Ours is an age that discounts the importance of that which cannot be seen. Emotional experiences are often judged to be merely "in our mind" and therefore not a part of the "real" world. Reality is the material world, that which can be seen or touched, that which has physical substance. Spiritual, emotional, and psychological experiences may be acknowledged, but they are relegated to a less real world, the world of mental experience. We are told that our fears are unreal because they have no rational basis. Elevators don't normally close in on a person and suffocate him, and therefore claustrophobia must be a product of our imagination, a mere mental reality. Similarly, emotional wounds are often judged to be mere mental phenomena and thus less real than physical wounds.

But although the emotional world is unseen, it is every bit as real as the physical one. It operates according to its own laws, which, while different from those in the physical realm, must be understood and respected if we are to live full and balanced lives. Just because emotions do not follow the laws of logic does not mean they are less real. The laws they follow are not logical, but psychological. And these laws can be discerned if we pay sufficient attention to the emotional aspects of our functioning. This is what we will do in the pages which follow. We will attempt to understand the psycho-logic of emotions, particularly as they occur in experiences of hurt.

This book has two major divisions. In part 1 we will consider the sorts of experiences in which we are usually hurt, examining these opportunities for hurt as they occur across the human life span. We will then trace the inner course of emotional events which predictably follow experiences of hurt. This will involve an examination of the ways in which we attempt to cope with hurts, focusing on some common but counterproductive coping strategies which actually impede healing.

While the bad news is that hurts seem to be an inevitable part of life, the good news is that they can be healed. In part 2 we will review what psychologists have come to understand about this process of emotional healing. The three chapters in this section will examine the emotional, intellectual, and volitional tasks that are involved in healing emotional wounds. Each will present concrete steps that can be taken to help ourselves and others come to experience this healing.

PART 1

The Context
of Emotional Wounds

1

The Hurts We Don't Deserve

As sparks fly upward, so man is born for trouble.

—Job

*The violation of personhood begins in the cradle,
if not in the womb.*

—Theodore Roszak

As presented in the Old Testament book bearing his name, Job's assessment of the inevitability of trouble in life is the response of a man who experiences undeserved pain of tragic proportions. But his assessment seems quite realistic. While some people certainly experience more hurt during their life than others, all of us receive hurts that we do not deserve. Vulnerability to emotional wounds is not the monopoly of any single age, ethnic, gender, or socioeconomic group. Each stage of life has its own unique emotional land mines and most of us stumble onto a number of these during the course of our lives.

Prenatal Emotional Wounds

Evidence suggests that our first experiences of emotional injury are usually in the first few months of life and often occur even before birth. It appears that the developing fetus is capable of experiencing emotional trauma and of retaining the effects of this trauma after birth. Psychologists interested in these prenatal emotional wounds suggest that such things as an unsuccessful attempt at an induced abortion or even the experience of residing within the womb of a woman who deeply resents the pregnancy may be emotionally traumatic for the fetus and may produce psychological consequences not unlike those associated with postnatal emotional trauma. These early emotional wounds were the focus of much of the research and treatment of the now-deceased British psychiatrist, Frank Lake, and healing of these wounds has been at the core of the work of the Clinical Theology Association, a British Christian counseling movement founded by him.[1]

The birth process itself can sometimes have negative emotional consequences; some problems in adulthood seem to be best understood as originating in a protracted or difficult birth. Reexperiencing these traumas, people often encounter strong feelings of terror or panic. Terror may be an emotional flashback to a long and difficult labor that was experienced by the fetus as entrapment within the birth canal. Similarly, panic may have been first experienced in response to choking or other difficulties in breathing immediately after birth. Intense feelings such as these may reappear in later life, springing as it were, from nowhere.[2]

As with the earlier fetal traumas, memories of these preverbal experiences are purely emotional. This is why they are so difficult to understand when they appear later in life. They seem to be irrational, but they are not irrational. They are merely *non*rational. The memory of these experiences is only a feeling memory. Due to the fact that the experience occurred before the development of language, there are no thoughts associated with

the feelings. However, since thoughts are usually primary in those experiences we think of as memories, we
often fail to recognize these emotional flashbacks as
memories and may attempt to discount the feelings
because we fail to understand them.

Stripped of any identifying thoughts, these feeling
memories are usually both very disturbing and very difficult to handle. When they come into our consciousness they often seem to sweep over us with a primitive
rage and fury. People frequently report feeling like helpless victims in the face of these waves of overwhelming
emotions that defy rational analysis or control. But we
do not have to be helpless in the face of these emotional
flashbacks. Understanding their source and meaning
does much to render them less disruptive, and healing
the underlying hurts is quite possible.

Childhood Emotional Wounds

While many people find these prenatal and birth traumas difficult to relate to, it is usually much easier to
identify with the hurts of childhood. Few people are
incapable of recalling at least some childhood hurts and
many more such wounds are obviously repressed and
forgotten.

One obvious source of childhood emotional damage
that is currently receiving a good deal of rightful attention is sexual abuse. Although estimates of the incidence of such abuse vary, current research suggests that
between 20 and 40 percent of females and between 10
and 25 percent of males are exposed to unwanted sexual
experiences as children.[3] Almost all of these children
show short-term emotional consequences of such abuse,
the most common problems including sleep disorders,
bedwetting, depression, anxiety, guilt, and increased
acts of aggression. Many also show long-term personali-

ty problems that extend well into adulthood, including drug and alcohol abuse, eating disorders, increased risk of suicidal behavior, and chronic low self-esteem. At least half of all runaway teens, young drug abusers, and prostitutes have been sexually abused, and approximately 5 percent of all adult females suffer impaired mental health directly attributable to childhood sexual abuse.

These statistics make abundantly clear the immense psychological and physical damage that is being done to children by sexually abusive adults. Healing of these wounds is possible but is often a complex process that requires professional help. Unfortunately, only a small percentage of these children get such help, the majority going through life impaired by the emotional consequences of these traumatic experiences.

Such major traumas as divorce or the death of a parent also have profound emotional consequences. Recent research on the effects of divorce on children suggest that long-term emotional problems are much more frequent than has usually been realized.[4] Less is known about the effects of the death of a parent on a child, although it appears that, depending on the age and psychological health of the child, long-term negative consequences of such a loss can be quite minimal. Short-term emotional pain is, however, an inevitable consequence of such a loss.

But apart from these more major traumas, many subtle experiences also wound the young and tender psyches of children. Ridicule, whether intentional or unintentional, always hurts, at least until we have experienced it so often that the scar tissue in this area is thick enough to mask the hurt. An alarmingly large percentage of all children hear repeated verbal put-downs from adults who are not able to recall their own childhood reactions to such emotional insults. Comments such as "You are going to turn out to be as worthless as your father," or "You idiot, you haven't got a brain in your head!" wound us long after we stop showing any reaction to them. They shape our self-image and often function as self-fulfilling prophecies, producing the very effects they were intended to discourage.

Even more subtle than ridicule are the many ways in which the spirits of children are broken. Sometimes this is the deliberate action of an adult who wishes to put a child in his or her place. With this intent, the adult then sets out to destroy the self-confidence of the child who is made to feel small, incompetent, or foolish. But more often this breaking of the child's spirit is unintentional. The adult may merely intend to set some limit, but ends up wounding the child.

A child can be told that he can't have candy before dinner and not feel that he has been criticized for asking for it. On the other hand, this information can be communicated with the same words but in a manner that hurts the child. He may feel foolish for having asked for the candy. Or he may be made to feel guilt or fear. In either case, he experiences hurt. But he also now feels less sure that the world is going to be a safe place for him. Consequently, it is most likely that he will be a little less trusting in his next transactions with this adult and probably with others as well.

Experiences of this sort are so common that some psychologists judge them to be an inevitable part of childhood. Fritz Kunkle, for example, feels that this is the origin of egocentricity.[5] He notes that children experience the hurt of a wounded spirit as a breach of trust. The oneness and trust that the child previously felt with the adult is now shattered and the child is consequently driven toward egocentricity. According to Kunkle, self-centeredness is a defense against the hurt associated with the experience of having our spirits broken as children. When this occurs, we will be forced to fight against this basic egocentricity for the rest of our lives.

The cruel remarks of other children can be another common source of hurts in childhood. Those who believe in the innocence of childhood have never carefully observed the interactions of children. The insults and abuses they give each other are limited only by their creativity, and sometimes an observing adult will be amazed by the degree of inventiveness demonstrated. Friendships often count for nothing as children turn upon each other with a cruelty seldom seen in adults. The intentionality present in the hurts one child inflicts upon another also makes them somewhat different from the hurts received at the hands of adults. Children usually intend to hurt each other with their insults or other acts of cruelty. And most often they succeed.

Adults often minimize the significance of these sorts of hurts by judging them to be quite minor emotional wounds. This is far from the truth. In fact, they often last a lifetime. A forty-three-year-old man recently told me of a wave of hurt and anger that swept over him on unexpectedly encountering a childhood bully whom he had not seen for thirty-five years! Pain which had been deeply buried away in a recessed corner of his mind suddenly burst into consciousness, and this childhood hurt was experienced once again with all the intensity that was present in the original experience. The part of him corresponding to the little seven-year-old boy he was when he experienced the hurt had retained this experience and had not grown or changed in any substantial way since it occurred.

The hurt experienced in interactions with childhood peers is very real. But the most significant damage to us lies deeper than the tender emotion; it lies in how we now come to view ourselves and others. Experiences with childhood peers set the stage for later adult relationships. These are basic building blocks of our personality. Emotional wounds in childhood are, therefore, never small or insignificant. They have more potential to affect us than those received during any other period of life.

Vulnerability to hurt in childhood is not limited to those who have bad parents or cruel friends. Because of the unreasonable expectations we tend to have of others and the emotional tenderness associated with our young and developing egos, we often take hurt even where none was, in fact, given. Of course, adults do this too, and in that case it reflects incomplete emotional development. But in children, particularly young children, it is to be expected.

Consider, for example, the infant. The crying of even the most contented baby often reveals a remarkable degree of demand and insistence. The message of the infant's cry is frequently, "I am hungry. I want to be fed, and I demand that you do it now!" But it is precisely such unreasonable demands as these which set the infant up for hurt. They come from the infant's feeling that the world revolves around him or her. Psychologists call this primary narcissism. No parent has a chance of being able to meet the expectations which seem to be held by the child during this stage of narcissism. The resulting hurts, called narcissistic injuries, occur in children regardless of how good, loving, or conscientious parents are. They are the by-products of the unreasonable expectations which are a part of this narcissistic stage of childhood. Parents are not responsible for these hurts and are really quite helpless to prevent them. But the hurts are still very real to the child.

Unrealistic expectations are also the source of hurts

of older children. Consider the five-year-old who responds to the presence of a new sibling with anger. It is quite likely that he also feels hurt when his mother spends time with the new baby, failing to give him her undivided attention. This emotional wound is self-inflicted; the child's expectations are the problem. Or consider the nine-year-old who is hurt by his teacher's failure to appropriately recognize what he considers to be an outstanding test score. Such a hurt is quite understandable and very real. However, its source lies in unrealistic expectations.

Adolescent Emotional Wounds

During adolescence, peers are usually the most significant sources of hurts. The breakup of romantic relationships, the insensitivity of a friend in the betrayal of a confidence, or the lack of loyalty of another are all the stuff of adolescent hurts. Adults often judge these emotional experiences of adolescence to be trivial, but they are far from trivial to the adolescent. In fact, because emotions tend to be rather raw during these often turbulent years, hurts are frequently experienced with more inner pain than that felt in any other period of life. The adolescent who says that he thought he would die in response to some shame-producing experience is probably describing his inner emotional experience fairly accurately. Adolescent emotional wounds are very real and their effects often reach well into adulthood.

Adolescents are also frequently hurt by their parents. Parents who give up trying to understand their adolescent children run the risk of judging them unfairly and hurting them. Having successfully negotiated the frequently difficult years of adolescence themselves, parents are often reluctant to once again enter the experience of this period of life with their children. Adding to the difficulty is the fact that the world of today's adolescent often seems very different from that which the adult faced, much more different than it actually is. Reluctance is then compounded with apprehension or even fear, and we are even less willing to attempt to enter the experience of our adolescents. But this usually sets us up for trouble. Standing back and watching our adolescents go through this period of life without attempting to understand and share their experiences is the soil that frequently produces conflict and hurt for both the adolescent and parent.

Adolescents are also hurt by themselves. Much like the younger child whose hurt is a result of unrealistic expectations of others, so too with adolescents hurt is often a natural consequence of the expectations they have of the world and how it ought to run. Idealism is a natural part of adolescence. But the idealistic values of the adolescent must be tempered by realism, and in this process hurt and disillusionment are quite common. Cynicism in adulthood is usually the result of wounded idealism in adolescence. Other people contribute to these wounds by being less than perfect. However, adolescent idealism sets the stage for these hurts.

Adult Emotional Wounds

The sources of hurt in adulthood are numerous. However, the core of the hurts in this period is the same as that of earlier ones—the perceived violation of trust. Trust can be violated in a great many ways. It may be an acquaintance criticizing me behind my back, a good friend forgetting my birthday or failing to call or visit during a period of sickness, or a spouse who is seemingly insensitive to my needs or feelings. In each case, however, the hurt has its source in the perception that someone who was trusted and from whom loyalty was expected has acted in disregard of that trust.

For many adults, the most significant hurts of this stage of life seem to occur within the context of marriage. The intimacy which is usually a part of marriage heightens the vulnerability to hurt. Greater intimacy means greater trust and this heightened trust leads to the increased capacity for hurt. However, because marriage is the closest adult equivalent to the parent-child relationship of childhood, it also tends to reactivate primitive expectations, feelings, and conflicts from childhood. Thus, marriage is a state of heightened vulnerability to hurt both because of the intimacy and the expectations which tend to be associated with it.

Beneath marital tensions is usually the sense on the part of one or both parties that trust has been violated. In fact, while it is common to seek the explanation for marital failure in personal incompatibility (i.e., few shared interests), external factors (i.e., an affair), or deficits in social skills (i.e., poor communication), the roots of marital failure more often are associated with a perceived violation of trust. Marital tensions usually mask marital disappointments and at the core of these disappointments is the perception of a violation of a trust.

Let me give you an example of how this works. Karen and Wayne had been married for six years and unhappy for the last three of those years. When they came for marital therapy they were each armed with a list of complaints about the other. But the problem really lay deeper than this. Beneath their anger at each other, they both also felt a good deal of hurt. Both perceived themselves to have been misunderstood by the other and to have been treated unfairly, and both felt that their trust had been violated.

The important thing to note about this violation of trust was that it had its origin in what we might think of as an implicit marital contract.[6] Both Karen and Wayne were operating on the basis of such an implicit contract which defined their respective marital roles and shaped their expectations of each other. In fact, they were not unique in this regard; all couples do the same. No matter how much the expectations each has of the other are explicitly discussed, important clauses of an implicit contract are always left uncommunicated. The disappointments that underlie marital tensions are based on these uncommunicated but firmly held expectations. And we respond to these expectations as if they were associated with an explicit contract that had been negotiated and accepted. Our disappointment is thus tainted with feelings of betrayal.

Karen was acting on the basis of her assumption that if her husband really loved her, he would know her needs without her having to tell him and would then set about to meet these needs. She experienced great hurt over the fact that Wayne did not seem to be very good at mind reading and she interpreted this as a violation of trust. He had, it seemed to her, failed to keep his end of the agreement. On the other hand, Wayne was acting on the basis of his assumption that Karen understood her role to be that of the strong one in the marriage, the one who would provide him with emotional support but would need little in return. He too felt that she had let him down by failing to keep her end of the bargain.

Neither Karen nor Wayne were very aware of these expectations. The implicit contract of their marriage was, for the most part, unconscious. However, this contract and the associated expectations clearly influenced their behavior. And these expectations were at the base of their respective feelings of a violation of trust. They both responded with hurt, anger, and disappointment based on the perception that their spouse had agreed to a certain contract for the marriage and then had failed to keep that agreement. This implicit contract had governed their expectations of and reactions to each other, and until it was made explicit and then renegotiated, the hurt and violation of trust that each experienced remained unintelligible and beyond healing.

These implicit contracts seem to be born out of our experiences of marriage and family life within our own families of origin. Many expectations come directly from what we observed in the interactions of our parents. If my father was sensitive to the emotional needs of my mother, there is a good chance that I will accept that as part of my expectation of what a husband does for his wife. However, if he treated her as a possession and regarded her emotional needs as a nuisance, then there is a good chance that these attitudes will shape my relationship with my wife.

Other expectations, however, are a conscious attempt to ensure that we do not repeat the pattern of our parents' marriage. For example, a woman may seek a husband who is more emotional than her father or a man may seek a woman who is more spontaneous and playful than his mother. But in each case, the expectations of what we should give and what we should receive from our spouse are substantially shaped by what we observed and experienced in our own families, particularly in relationships with our opposite sex parent.[7]

This does not mean that our marital expectations, conscious or unconscious, are determined by our childhood experiences. However, they are influenced and shaped by what we observe and experience about families, particularly in our own family of origin. These sources of influence seem to have the greatest effect when they are beyond our awareness. To become aware of the things that influence us is to begin to diminish their potency. To become aware, therefore, of the extent to which I react to my spouse as if he or she were my opposite sex parent is to begin to encounter my spouse as my spouse and not as my parent.

Once again, therefore, we often contribute to our own hurt by the expectations we adopt. Some of these expectations are close to conscious awareness and are readily available for our examination. Others are more unconscious and difficult to examine. Thoughtful reflection on our behavior will, however, reveal our expectations and allow us to modify the most unrealistic ones. This is a very good way of preventing some of the hurts which would otherwise come our way.

While this sort of perceived violation of trust is the basis of most marital problems, there are obviously a good many even more direct ways in which marital trust can be violated. An extramarital affair is the classic form of this violation. Other forms of marital unfaithfulness—such as no longer treating the other with respect, or failing to honor commitments for a primacy of marital love over love of job, children, or friends—also have the same disastrous emotional effects. Trust is also violated when lies replace truthfulness, manipulation replaces mutuality, or emotional isolation replaces intimacy. In each case, hurt is the result of a violation of trust.

But while marriage is a major context of hurts in adulthood, the married do not have a monopoly on hurts in this period of life. Singles are also vulnerable to hurts, many of which involve disappointments in romantic relationships. This may involve a partner who is not interested in commitment and who uses others for sex, status, or other temporary pleasures. Or it may be a hurt received in a relationship with someone who is ideal but who rejects love. These and other hurts in romantic relationships may lead the single person away from such attachments to opposite sex and sometimes even same sex friendships. And once again, the source of the hurt is the perceived betrayal of trust.

While married adults are vulnerable to hurt in work relationships as well as personal ones, singles are sometimes even more vulnerable to hurt in the vocational context. Single adults who retreat from romantic relationships may turn to their work for fulfilment. In so doing, however, they may be setting themselves up for hurt by virtue of the high expectations they have for their jobs. People who are perceived to get in the way of realizing these expectations are easily identified, therefore, with the hurt and disappointment.

Intentionality and Hurt

In considering these examples of emotional hurt, it should be noted that hurt can be communicated regardless of whether it is intended or not. Intentional hurt has its own unique sting. However, much of the time we assume intentionality and react as if this is the case. This means that the hurt that we experience is not usually effected by the actual intentionality of the other person.

It is quite clear, however, that some people are too thin-skinned. They routinely take offense where none was intended and where none should be taken. Sometimes such a sensitivity to hurt comes from previous traumas. Real and significant hurts make us more emotionally sensitive and sometimes leave us vulnerable to taking hurt where none is intended. We frequently say that such people read too much into the situation. The real problem is that they tend to read situations only from their own perspective. Their vulnerability to hurt reflects a difficulty in getting outside of their own perspective and into that of another.

The hurts resulting from such heightened emotional sensitivity are very real. The hurt is not any less, nor is it made up or unreal. It is, however, tragic in that the situation need not have been experienced as hurtful. But the hurt is real. Hurt can come from a *perceived* violation of trust, as well as from an actual violation of trust. My trust may be violated without my being aware of it. In such a case, I will not experience hurt. On the other hand, no actual violation of trust may have occurred and yet I will experience hurt if I perceive such a violation to have occurred.

Hurts occur on the inner stage. Although they are obviously related to external events, they are not a part of this outer world. Therefore we cannot expect them to follow the rules of this external world. This is why hurt can be present and real even when no hurt was intended. Similarly, this is why hurt can be experienced even when nothing objectively hurtful occurred in the external world of behavior and events. All that must occur is the perceived violation of a trust.

The Intimate Enemy

We are hurt more by friends than by strangers. Friends are capable of hurting us both more easily and more deeply. Just as rape and other crimes of violence are most likely among people who already know each other, life's most significant emotional wounds are usually from those in our circle of family, friends, and intimate contacts.

The reason is quite simple. We invest these people with a level of trust and expectation that we do not generally bestow on strangers. Thus, if I am robbed by a stranger, I may feel anger but I will not likely experience the depth of hurt associated with betrayal by a friend. The trusted friend has to do much less in order for me to experience his actions as hurtful. And when the source of hurt is a major betrayal by a friend or family member, the hurt is as deep as can be humanly experienced. We do not expect much from the stranger. Therefore, if we are treated badly, we have not set ourselves up to be hurt through our expectations. From friends, however, we expect a good deal more. This is why our greatest vulnerability to hurt is with those within our inner circle of personal relationships.

This is not to say that we cannot be hurt by a stranger. While we trust strangers less than friends and generally expect less from them, we do expect them to relate to us with common decency and a respect for our rights. Thus, if we are treated unfairly or our rights are violated, we experience hurt. The victim of a robbery may experience considerable hurt in such an incident. One such person, responding to a forcible entry of his home, told me of the sense of violation that he experienced over the incident. He felt as if he, not his house, had been violated. Although nothing of value was taken, he felt the loss of something quite important within himself. His basic sense of safety had been diminished and this was at the core of his experience of hurt.

Who Is to Blame?

Finally, the examples of hurt which we have considered also illustrate the fact that while our hurts are experienced in interactions with others, sometimes we are the cause of our own woundedness. We sometimes shoot ourselves in the foot, so to speak, by adopting unrealistic expectations about how others should treat us. As we examine our expectations of others and modify the most unrealistic aspects of these, we eliminate some of the potential hurts which await us.

This realization should also help us as we think about the hurt others experience in relation to us. Sometimes I am directly responsible for other people's pain. In these circumstances it may be appropriate for me to seek their forgiveness, and this will often be an essential part of healing the hurt and the relationship. However, on other occasions I should recognize the ways in which other people have contributed to their own hurts and not attempt to take the full responsibility for those hurts. It may then be possible for me to help the other person recognize his or her inappropriate expectations which contributed to the experience of disappointment and hurt.

Vulnerability and Humanness

No one likes to be hurt. We recoil from emotional pain just as naturally as we do from physical pain. However, in spite of the steps we may take to emotionally protect ourselves from the vicissitudes of life, we remain susceptible to hurt. If we somehow manage to eliminate all vulnerability, we will have also managed to eliminate our humanness.

To be a person is to be vulnerable. The more invulnerable we become, the more impersonal we become. Machines cannot be hurt and the more we succeed in eliminating the potential for hurt, the more we function in a machinelike manner.

But such machinelike functioning has negative consequences for us and for others. We may lessen the chances of hurt by such a posture. However, at the same time we also sacrifice joy, wonder, excitement, and a host of other positive emotional experiences. Humans seem to be incapable of shutting down just one type of emotional experience. The avoidance of vulnerability through the adoption of an impersonal style of living inevitably involves the loss of all emotional experience.

As we relate to others in a machinelike manner, we fashion them in the same mold. Consequently, we also hurt them, not just ourselves. Personal relationships foster the development of persons while impersonal relationships foster the development of impersonal beings. The choice to adopt the invulnerability of an impersonal style of life and relationship has the effect of pulling others down to that level as well. To lose vulnerability is to lose a good deal more than the risk of hurt.

The relationship between personhood and vulnerability can also be seen in the character of God. God is a person—not a human person, but still a person. This is one important way in which we, made in his image, reflect aspects of his nature and being. We are persons only because God is a person.

As a person, God is also vulnerable to hurt. Along with other emotions such as love, rage, and jealousy, God is described in the Scriptures as being grieved by those who reject him. Recall Jesus crying over Jerusalem because of the city's rejection of him and his message. And even more powerfully, recall his own experience of the rejection of his Father when he cried out in anguish on the cross, "My God, my God! Why hast thou forsaken me?" Or consider Jesus' betrayal at the hands of Judas, a member of his inner circle of closest friends. If it is impossible for God to avoid the experience of emotional wounds, on what basis do we expect our lot to be any better?

To be a person is to be susceptible to hurt, and to be a human person is to be even more vulnerable. To be a human person in a fallen world and relating to other sinful persons is, then, to be in an environment where hurts are the norm, not the exception.

Suffering and Spirituality

But the Christian has a unique hope in the experience of hurt. While we might wish that our life in Christ would guarantee that we will escape emotional or physical hurt, it is obvious that this is not the Christian hope. Peter Bertocci notes that the question is not "Shall we suffer?" but "For what shall we suffer?" and he goes on to argue that the greatest benefit of the Christian faith is that it gives us an answer to this question.[8] Christian faith gives us a reason to suffer and a context within which we can understand this suffering. The Christian hope is that in suffering we can uniquely encounter Christ, the suffering Son of God.

Most of us would prefer to identify with Christ in his success. Since he has also shared these experiences, he can identify with us in them and we can expect to meet him in their midst. However, this is not where we are told that we ought to expect to encounter him most fully. Rather, it is in suffering. The Christian's comfort in suffering is the knowledge that our Savior suffers with us. And in this knowledge, I receive a unique measure of his grace. Even as he was made perfect through suffering, so I, encountering him, face the possibility of growth unavailable to me apart from suffering. This is both the mystery and hope of suffering, and it should serve as a great comfort to all Christians who suffer and face the inevitability of doing so again in the future.

To speak of the possibility of good coming out of hurt is not to make hurt a good. However, for the Christian, hurt can be transformed, and consequently my attitude toward it can likewise be transformed. As I come to see hurt as a unique opportunity to encounter God and receive his grace I am able to begin to move from despair to acceptance. I may not be able to control whether or not I experience hurt, but I can begin to control how I respond to it. This, in turn, makes healing of the hurt much more possible.

Summary

This review of the ways in which we are emotionally hurt throughout life confirms the realism of the words of Job with which we began this chapter. We seem, indeed, to be born for trouble. Emotional wounds are an inevitable part of life. The question is not whether we will be hurt, but how we will react.

In the next chapter we will examine both the inner mental and outer behavioral responses to hurt. What we will see is that the typical reaction to an emotional wound is a complex interaction of feelings of sadness and anger. Understanding the psychology of emotional pain is essential if we are to react to hurts in ways that promote healing rather than in ways that impede such healing.

2

The Psychology of Emotional Pain

Two chambers has the heart. There dwelling, live Joy and Pain apart.

—Hermann Neumann

In the last chapter, I described emotional hurt as the result of a perceived violation of our trust, including a violation of our rights or sense of fairness. We feel hurt if people act in such a way as to betray the trust we have placed in them. We also feel hurt if someone fails to respect our rights or doesn't play by the rules because we had trusted that we would be treated fairly. These violations of trust may be intentional or unintentional, trivial or major, real or imagined. Regardless, the response to such a perceived violation of trust is an experience of hurt.

But what exactly is this experience of hurt? Thus far I have used the term rather generally. It is now time to look more closely at this concept and try to understand what is involved in emotional pain. What we will discover is that perceived violations of trust set in motion a chain of inner events which, when combined, we experience as hurt.

Loss

The first response to the experience of hurt is a sense of loss. It is common for this loss to be covered by anger so quickly that most people are unaware that it is a part of their response to hurt. However, it is a very important part of the whole process—so important, in fact, that we cannot gain freedom from the anger without facing this underlying sense of loss.

Emotional wounds always leave us with some diminishment of our sense of self. It may be a loss of self-esteem or possibly of our sense of self-competence or worth. However, the first response to emotional hurt seems to be to experience the violation as something having been taken away from me.

As an example of this, consider Linda's response to the betrayal by her executive assistant. She and this assistant had worked together for three years and had known each other for several more before that. Linda had invited the assistant to join her in the firm just after she had been made a partner. Since that time they had come to trust each other implicitly and their business relationship, as well as their personal one, had been good.

Recently, Linda discovered that her assistant had been embezzling money from the firm almost since her first day on the job. Linda was unable to believe this until she was confronted with hard proof collected by the police. Her first conscious emotion was rage. She was overwhelmed with anger and, acting on this, fired her assistant immediately. However, when the anger continued to plague her two months after the incident, she consulted a psychotherapist for help in dealing with her feelings.

The reason she was stuck in her anger was that she

had not allowed herself to acknowledge or experience her losses. Her sense of loss was so painful that she, like most of us, could not tolerate it for very long. This was why it was followed so quickly by feelings of anger which served as a defense against the more basic experience of loss. Although anger was a painful emotional state, it was preferable to the feeling of loss which it covered.

But what was her loss? It took Linda some time to discover the answer to this question, and what she discovered was that she had experienced the breach of trust by her assistant as taking a number of most valuable things from her. First, she became aware that she had lost a large portion of her trust of people. She had always been a very trusting person, possibly even somewhat naively so. This quality had, however, made her a good manager because she had always been able to see the best in others and help them act on their potential. It was not just that Linda could no longer trust her assistant; she felt shaken to her core by the realization that her basic way of viewing and relating to others now had to be reexamined.

Linda also discovered that she had lost much of her sense of competence. She felt like a fool. Her belief in her assistant and her failure to have had even a momentary suspicion of her during the whole time the assistant had been coordinating the investigation of the missing funds now made her feel foolish and incompetent. This was a great loss because it stood in stark contrast to the considerable self-confidence she had previously felt in her work with people.

The dominant feelings associated with this experience of loss are those of vulnerability and sadness. These were very much a part of Linda's experience and they almost invariably accompany the sort of losses that

are involved in emotional hurt. But another feeling that
often accompanies hurt is a feeling of being alone, of
being abandoned or isolated. These feelings give particularly clear evidence of how central loss is to the experience of hurt.

The events of the last few days of Jesus' life on earth
provide a good illustration of this. Jesus shared a final
Passover meal with his disciples knowing that within
hours one of them would betray him while another
would claim that he never knew him. At this meal Jesus
was also confronted with the discouraging evidence of
how little spiritual progress the disciples had made,
hearing yet another argument among them about who
would be counted by history as the greatest. Immediately
after this, Jesus took them to the garden of Gethsemane,
where he asked them to wait with him while he prayed.
All of them fell asleep, failing to comfort him in his
hours of deep agony. He woke them up, asking them to
pray with him, only to have them fall asleep once again.
Quickly on the heels of this he was betrayed by Judas,
abandoned by Peter, arrested, beaten, mocked, and crucified, all of this leading up to his heartrending cry from
the cross, "My God, my God, why have you forsaken
me?" (Matt. 27:46).

This primal cry of utter abandonment comes across
the centuries to remind us how desperately alone Jesus
felt on the cross. His hurt was experienced primarily in
terms of loss. This pure and essential core of hurt was
not, in Jesus, contaminated with anger or any other
defensive reaction. His emotional reaction was uncomplicated, but, because of this, it was much more raw. It
was simply and purely the experience of abandonment.

Jesus' feeling of abandonment was first and foremost
the loss of the experience of intimacy with his Father.
But he also faced the loss of fellowship with his disci-

ples (including the hurt associated with the experience of betrayal and denial), the end of his mission on earth (with so many visible signs of it having not been much of a success), and the loss of his life. Is it any wonder that we are told that his soul was grieved to the point of death?

The pain associated with the experience of abandonment by a loved one, particularly a person on whom one depends for one's very existence, is probably as intense as emotional pain gets. But even when the feeling of abandonment is not a part of the experience of hurt, the sense of loss is. This loss, whatever it may be, must be mourned if we are to avoid getting stuck in the depression that accompanies this first stage of emotional hurt. Much like the process of mourning the death of a loved one, losses of any sort must be grieved before we are emotionally free to leave them behind. Such grieving was very much a part of Jesus' reaction to his losses. Later we will explore what such grieving involves, but here we should note that as the perfect example of fully functioning humanity, Jesus' reaction to loss exemplifies the healing way to respond to life's deepest hurts.

Anger

Feelings of loss, and the vulnerability that usually accompanies them, are so tender that few people are able to tolerate them for long. For most people, feelings of anger quickly replace them. For some people, the feelings of anger are automatic and they never consciously experience the feelings of loss. In either case, however, anger helps us defend against the more painful feelings of loss by serving as a distraction. Our focus is now on the other person who has hurt us rather than on ourselves.

Sue's immediate response to her recent experience of

rape was overwhelming waves of hatred and rage. It was not until much later that she could face the more painful feelings of shame and loss. All she was aware of at first was a need to retaliate, a desire to find the man who had raped her and somehow hurt him so badly that he would never be the same again. She was preoccupied with this retaliatory fantasy. It seemed actually to soothe her. She would go to sleep thinking about what she would do to him if she caught up with him and would often wake up in the morning with the same thoughts in her mind.

Sue's anger was not serving her well. Anger can be a very constructive force when it mobilizes us to action in response to some injustice or evil. However, in Sue's case, she would never act on the anger in the way she fantasized. It was just a distraction for her pain. It was not that she did not have a right to feel angry. She did, and the eventual healing of the emotional wounds from the rape would require her to face and work through these feelings. But as real and legitimate as they were, they were at this point getting in the way and were, therefore, destructive.

This is the way feelings of anger usually function in the early stages of any emotional hurt. We want to act, to retaliate in some way. But what we really need to do is *feel*. The feelings of anger must be faced head-on if they are to be resolved. Failure to do so results in the anger being managed in some destructive manner, either through inappropriate expression,which hurts others, or through repression, which hurts ourselves.

Because anger is so easily expressed inappropriately, it has frequently been condemned by Christians. But what we fail to recognize when we do so is that anger, as a God-given dynamic of personality, existed before the fall. The fall didn't create anything; it merely distorted that which was already present. Anger is not a product of sin. Like the rest of human personality, anger (or at least the capacity for anger) was a part of the original good creation of God that was subsequently distorted by sin.

God's intention is not to repress and hide these effects of sin but to restore us to a state of wholeness. God is not in the business of sweeping problems under the carpet. He is in the business of renewal and transformation. Our job, therefore, is to work alongside of him in this work of restoration. Anger shouldn't be eliminated; it should be redeemed. This involves understanding the creational role of anger in personality, discerning the distorting effects of sin, and then, with God's assistance, working to restore anger to its proper place and expression.[1]

Briefly, anger can be viewed as the fuel that energizes us to respond to situations that demand action but to which we might otherwise respond only with passivity or avoidance. It is anger, combined with judgment, that allows us to declare with God things to be "not good" and then to take the necessary steps to remedy the situation. Anger is, therefore, a constructive part of our response to hurt when it leads us to seek, not retaliation, but correction of the injustice. Anger is constructively engaged when, therefore, we report crimes to the police and persevere in actions that ensure a just response on their part. It is similarly engaged in a constructive way when we confront friends who violate a commitment or in some way betray us.

Two Sides of a Coin

Sadness and anger are the two complementary faces of the experience of emotional hurt. However, because it is difficult to sustain both feelings at the same time, we usually respond to hurt by alternating between the two feelings. For a while we are self-preoccupied and aware to some extent of the damage we have sustained in the experience of hurt. In this stage we experience sadness and, quite possibly, actual depression. We feel acutely vulnerable to further hurt and feel the need to retreat to some safe corner of our world. These feelings are the primary emotional consequences of loss.

But then the pain gets too intense and we end our introspection by shifting our attention to the one who has hurt us. In so doing we move from sad to angry feelings. Anger is thus a secondary emotional consequence of hurt. It serves as a defense against the sadness by helping us gain some distance from the hurt. However, the hurt does not get healed by our focus on the anger; eventually sad feelings again press their way into consciousness and we return to the first stage.

People can get stuck in either of these stages. Chronic depression is the result of getting stuck in the feelings of loss. Such persons feel their loss very deeply. They often describe their experience in terms which suggest that something vital has been taken from them. They shut down their emotions in order to no longer feel the hurt and pain. But in shutting down pain and other negative emotions they shut down all emotions, and the lack of life that they experience is a direct result of this action on their part. They also tend to withdraw from other people and, consequently, feel increasingly estranged from others and themselves. Their life becomes more and more filled with despair and self-pity until they become so comfortable with their depression that they prefer it to restored life. Ironically, their depression has become so much a part of them that, while it is still a source of great pain, it has become a stable and almost comfortable component of their identity.

As tragic as this scenario is, it is not uncommon. It is well illustrated in the life of a man I shall call Ralph. I first saw this thirty-one-year-old man after his wife made an appointment for him and told him that if he did not come and see me she would leave him. Nine months prior to this contact he had been fired from his job. He had never gotten over this event. He had been an operating room assistant in a major university hospital and had liked his work and done very well in it. However, he was evidently falsely accused of stealing drugs from the hospital and was dismissed from his position. Initially he felt murderous rage at the person who had dismissed him. However, over time he turned this anger more and more in upon himself. Depression was the result.

For the first two months after his dismissal his wife accepted the fact that he did not look for a new job. She understood that he felt emotionally overwhelmed and they agreed that he needed a break. However, as month followed month and he made no attempt to pick up the pieces of his life and move on, she became more and more concerned about him.

When I saw Ralph, he told me he had no desire to live. He assured me that he was not actively suicidal, but neither was he willing or desirous of actively pursuing life. He felt broken by the job dismissal and told me that his life had ended with that event. He resented both being forced to see me and his wife's efforts to help him. Although his life was miserable, he wanted to remain depressed. He felt it was his right to do so and argued that no one else could tell him how he should feel. His rights had previously been violated and now he stood firmly on his right to be miserable.

Getting stuck in the anger stage of a response to hurt is equally tragic and even more common. One of the reasons this is such a trap is that feelings of anger often serve to empower us. When one's response to hurt is a feeling of vulnerability and powerlessness, anger provides a restoration of one's sense of power. This makes it very seductive. Also, as pointed out earlier, anger serves as a distraction from the hurt and this is an additional and quite substantial payoff.

Tragically, psychotherapy sometimes seems to encourage people to get stuck in the anger stage. Because it is quite common for counselors and therapists to see people who are smiling on the outside but seething with rage inside, they frequently find themselves encouraging those they seek to help to get in touch with their anger. And most of the time this is quite necessary for emotional healing. However, the expression of anger is only the means to the end, not the end itself. Sadly, some people do get stuck at just this point, leaving therapy angry and often quite obnoxious. Forgiveness is the antidote to this problem. But unfortunately, this concept has not had much currency in psychology.[2]

Getting stuck in feelings of either loss or anger is a defense against the opposite set of feelings. People who can tolerate feelings of anger often have great difficulty experiencing feelings of sadness or hurt, and thus they use anger to ward off feelings of hurt. Similarly, feelings of sadness and loss are more comfortable for other people than feelings of anger, and these individuals often unconsciously choose depression as a way to ward off the more disruptive feelings of anger.

In order for the healing of hurt to occur, we must have some degree of tolerance for both sets of feelings. Sadness and anger are both usually a part of the experience of hurt. If we need to deny either one, we will end up being stuck in the other.

The Masks of Anger

Some people express their anger in a rather direct manner. They may relate to others in a bitter or even malicious way, or they may be quick-tempered or chronically vindictive. In such cases it is not difficult to recognize that they have experienced hurts over which they are still angry. However, the expression of anger is often much more subtle. It can appear in many different guises, each of which masks to some extent the essential core of anger.

I have already pointed out that depression is often a disguised form of anger. Chronic depression or depression that is disproportionate to the precipitating cause usually reflects masked anger. Depression is the result of anger turned in upon oneself. While this is not the only cause of depression,[3] it does seem to be a dynamic of most experiences of depression, even those depressive illnesses that seem to be physiologically based. The person who feels depressed is often a person who tends to repress anger. This does not eliminate the anger; it merely pushes it out of consciousness. Inevitably, however, the feelings of anger reappear in some disguised form, and often that is depression.

Nowhere is the relationship between depression and anger more clear than in the case of suicide. Acts of violence are always an expression of anger, and suicide is no exception. It is not merely an act of desperation; it is an act of violent hostility. The primary target for this hostility is the suicidal person. However, it is sometimes also directed toward those who will be hurt by the death and will, perhaps, be punished by feelings of guilt or sorrow. Regardless of the specific meaning behind the act, it is clearly an act of hostility.

Suspicion is another common mask of anger. While caution may sometimes be an appropriate way of relating to others, chronic suspicion is usually an indirect expression of unresolved anger. The chronically suspicious person projects his anger indiscriminately onto others. He is then plagued with the perception that others feel toward him as he does toward them. In the most extreme forms of suspicion, a person believes that others are plotting his destruction. When these feelings have no basis in reality they are called paranoid delusions and are a symptom of a serious mental disorder. In less extreme forms the person is routinely suspicious of others and has great trouble trusting anyone. In either case, chronic suspiciousness reflects underlying displaced anger.

Suspiciousness and mistrust are responses to unresolved hurts. Unfortunately, however, persons prone to suspicion no longer feel the hurt or are aware of the connection between past experiences and current behavior. They fail, therefore, to correctly understand their experiences. The issue is not the trustworthiness of others, rather it is their own tendency to avoid underlying hurts. This results in their being controlled by these hurts.

Jealousy is frequently also a mask for anger. This does not mean that all jealousy is reducible to anger. Moderate levels of jealousy can be an appropriate response toward an object of love. However, chronic jealousy almost always reflects repressed anger.

The relationship between jealousy and anger is suggested by the fact that jealousy is very frequently a symptom among people suffering from paranoid disorders. The more paranoid a person is, the more jealous he or she usually feels toward loved ones. But the actions that grow out of a jealous spirit betray the underlying hostility. No one knows this better than the person who is the object of the jealousy. The jealous friend or lover makes the loved one's life miserable by the expressions of jealousy and this clearly betrays the underlying anger.

Self-pity is another indirect expression of anger. Like

depression, this is a result of anger being repressed and then turned back upon the self. The result is a whining manner of relating to others that serves as a self-fulfiling prophecy. The self-pitying individual becomes less and less attractive to others and subsequently other people begin to back away from him. This then confirms the expectation of the one pitying himself. He now has proof that he is a victim of an unfair world that is organized around a plan to keep him oppressed and unhappy. The individual who pities himself quickly becomes, therefore, a pitiable person.

Impatience is also a by-product of anger. Here the veneer is thinner and somewhat more transparent because the impatient individual is overtly angry much of the time. Such a person may lean on the horn in a traffic jam, express irritation at a checkout clerk in a grocery store who makes an error, or yell at the dog if it does not relieve itself quickly enough.

Impatient people seem to get angry easily. The actual amount of anger expressed in any one situation may be quite small. However, the objects of anger are clearly scapegoats.

Cynicism is also built on a core of anger. The cynic can no longer trust things to be as they appear. Hope is judged to be mere sentimentalism and belief is judged to be naive. Truth is viewed as a personal creation and its value disparaged. No longer being able to enjoy life personally, the cynic seeks to poison it for others and rob them of any beauty or joy they might otherwise experience. This is, of course, quite a hostile act.

Another mask of anger is passive-aggressive behavior. As the name implies, passive-aggressive behavior expresses hostility in a passive or indirect manner. An example would be a person who is chronically late for commitments with people, particularly people who are somewhat obsessive about punctuality. This behavior is an indirect way of expressing resentment. However, when such individuals are confronted with this resentment, they will usually deny any such feelings, providing elaborate rationalizations for their behavior.

Adolescence is the period of life where such behaviors are performed with the highest levels of creativity. Teenage pregnancies or clashes with the law sometimes serve these passive-aggressive purposes. When this is the case, such individuals deny personal responsibility for their behavior and its consequences. However, if they are honest, they will admit that they take secret delight in the pain they are causing their parents or others. Such behaviors reflect obvious hostility.

One of the most creative examples of passive-aggressive behavior I have seen was demonstrated by a twelve-year-old boy who was furious with his adoptive parents but who, at the same time, was afraid to show his anger to them. He related to these parents with superficial pleasantness but was always doing things to make their life unpleasant. He would offer to wash the dishes and then would invariably break the most expensive piece of china. He would then apologize profusely and would offer some explanation in which he attempted to remove the blame from himself. When his parents stopped letting him wash dishes, he would ask to help in some other way and would again wreak havoc in that area. His piece de resistance involved cleaning up after the family dog had an accident on the carpet but hiding the towels in the air conditioning system. Four days later, when his parents finally found the source of the odor permeating the house, they brought their son to me for help. In spite of his protestations of denial, it wasn't hard to identify the problem as hidden anger.

These are a few of the many faces of anger. With one

or more of these faces, anger always shows itself to be a part of the experience of hurt. But equally important are the feelings of loss which the anger masks. A movement back and forth between feelings of loss and those of anger is the normal response to the experience of emotional hurt.

Psychological Trauma

At several points I have described major sources of hurt as traumas. Much of the psychological study of emotional hurts has focused upon these major traumas. In order to further understand the psychology of emotional hurts, let us briefly consider what we know about human response to trauma.

One leading expert on psychological trauma has defined it as any overwhelming emotion that makes a person feel a loss of faith that there is safety, order, or continuity in life.[4] Trauma is thus defined not so much in terms of external events but rather in terms of the person's response to these events. An event is traumatic for a given individual if it results in that person losing the sense of having a safe place to retreat to in dealing with the frightening emotions he is facing. This definition is broad enough to include both interpersonal traumas, such as rape, incest, or betrayal, and impersonal traumas, such as fires, floods, or accidents. The response to both these major categories of trauma is almost identical and has been noted following combat trauma, rape, kidnapping, spouse abuse, natural disasters, accidents, concentration camp experiences, incest, burns, and child abuse.

Much like the emotional hurts discussed earlier in this chapter, our response to major forms of trauma again involves an alternation between two experiences. In the case of major traumas, these are reexperiencing the trauma and emotional numbness.

The most dramatic forms of reexperiencing the traumatic event involve nightmares and flashbacks. In these experiences the person faces all the terror of the original trauma over and over again. In less severe forms, reexperiencing involves obsessive daytime rumination on the events of the trauma. Such rumination is not under voluntary control. In fact, the trauma victim usually wishes for nothing more than to be able to stop experiencing these intrusive and disruptive thoughts. However, they sweep over him with relentless fury and leave him continuously preoccupied with the trauma and its pain.

The reexperiencing stage leaves a person with overwhelming feelings of helplessness, apprehension, and panic. Most individuals also experience an increase of energy manifested in irritability, hyperactivity, and aggression.

Because of the great pain associated with reexperiencing the trauma, periods of reexperiencing alternate with periods of emotional numbness. As the name suggests, emotional numbness involves a shutting down of all emotions. This stage also tends to involve social isolation and a resulting sense of estrangement. Depression is more prominent during this phase, although it is not absent from the reexperiencing phase. Psychosomatic symptoms are also common. The result is a robotlike existence designed to ward off memories of the trauma.

The two phases of reexperiencing and emotional numbness alternate until the trauma is resolved or the person's functioning has restabilized. This cycle of feelings parallels the alternation between anger and sadness associated with less severe emotional wounds. However, unlike these less severe emotional hurts where people can get stuck in one or the other of the two phases, the person who has experienced a major psychological trauma tends to be propelled through this alternating cycle of stages until restabilization of personality occurs.

Restabilization is said to occur when the individual is capable of once again resuming the normal responsibilities and routines of life. In most cases this does not yet involve resolution of the trauma. The alternation of emotional numbness and reexperiencing is replaced by a less intense but more continuous emotional numbing, and the person is able to once again get on with life. However, apart from eventual resolution of the trauma, long-term effects such as generalized nervousness and apprehension, chronic physical illness, alcoholism or drug dependence, a tendency to dissociation, and a chronic sense of helplessness are all common.[5]

Resolution of the trauma usually takes years and often requires professional help. Resolution is judged to have occurred when the individual can recall the trauma at will without adverse emotional pain while at the same time being equally capable of turning his or her mind to other matters. Memory of the trauma will remain, but the sting of the experience should now be only a dull pain. Because victims of psychological trauma may return to a semblance of normal life even though they are in fact still suffering from significant continuing effects, it is often hard to tell when resolution has occurred. But some degree of resolution is, in fact, possible. It is not necessary to go through life in bondage to the crippling effects of these major traumas.

Time Heals, Doesn't It?

Perhaps you feel that I am making too much of the hurts which we experience in life. Possibly you are saying something like, "Granted we all get hurt from time to time, but time itself is the great healer. Just get on with life and the hurts will eventually disappear."

Even if you are not tempted to count on time to take care of hurts, it is quite apparent that most people are. Consider how frequently such advice is given. We are encouraged to wait for time, the reputed great physician, to heal our hurts. Our part in the process is quite passive. All we have to do is wait.

But does it work this way? Unfortunately, it does not. The reality is that time is necessary but not sufficient in the healing process. Healing takes time but it also requires much more of an active response on the part of the one who is hurting. When we count on time to produce healing, what we receive is not genuine healing but rather the elimination of feelings through repression, denial, or some other mental mechanism of defense.

In chapter 1 I mentioned the man who unexpectedly encountered a childhood bully and suddenly felt all the rage and emotional pain that had been his experience as a young child. He thought these feelings had all been healed. He had not even thought about this individual for more than thirty years! How could such feelings remain alive for such a long time and yet be completely beyond awareness?

Band Aids That Block Healing

One of the most remarkable features of the human mind is our incredible capacity to forget, ignore, or in other ways avoid things that trouble us. We do this by means of defense mechanisms which operate unconsciously and serve to block conscious awareness of troublesome experiences and feelings. These defenses allow us to live with the pain, conflicts, and traumas that are an inevitable part of life. And for this we can be thankful. However, while they help us cope, they also have a major negative side effect—they also block growth and healing by distorting reality or in some way letting us avoid it. When we count on the passage of time to remove the sting of the hurts we experience, we are counting on the mental mechanisms of defense to help us forget. We should never confuse this with genuine healing.

Denial

The first line of defense against emotional wounds is often denial. By means of this defense we are able to pretend that experiences simply did not happen. This is not a matter of consciously deciding to pretend. Denial, like all our other defense mechanisms, operates unconsciously. Although it is one of the most simple defenses, it is remarkably powerful. In fact, it is sufficiently strong that it provides us with a distorted perception of reality, one that conforms to our wishes.

Denial takes the form of refusing to consciously acknowledge important aspects of one's experience, usually things associated with unwanted feelings or thoughts. We speak of someone being in denial if they do not yet accept the reality of the death of a loved one or if they fail to emotionally acknowledge a diagnosis of a terminal illness in themselves. But denial is more commonly directed toward experiences or feelings which are incongruent with one's self-concept or values.

This perhaps helps us understand why denial is so commonly employed by Christians as a way of dealing with feelings that they judge inappropriate. Thus, for example, someone may believe that Christians should not get depressed. Because feelings of depression might be judged to be indicative of sin or possibly of a lack of faith, such feelings are simply eliminated from consciousness. When such a person feels what others would call depression, he must, therefore, deny this fact.

Another example of a religious use of denial is the inappropriate quotation of Scripture as a way of masking painful feelings. A person might, for example, react to the death of a loved one with a glib "the Lord giveth and the Lord taketh away," or to some personal catastrophe with "all things work together for good to them who love the Lord." To call this denial is not to dispute the reality of these precious truths. It is, however, to point to the abuse of Scripture that is involved in such magical use of the Word of God to ward off deep pain that should be experienced if it is to be healed. God promises us comfort in our trials; he doesn't tell us to pretend that the experiences we face are not, in fact, trying.

Like many defense mechanisms, denial can be an aid to short-term coping with events which are otherwise overwhelming. What we call being in shock in response to bad news is this mechanism of denial. In such a situation, denial is of great help. It allows us to retain our equilibrium and accept the reality of the unwanted experience more slowly. But if denial, rather than simply cushioning us against unpleasant experiences, blocks them out completely, then healing is also blocked.

Repression

Denial is seldom powerful enough to completely block out unwanted experiences for the long term. Usually that which we deny has a way of seeping back into consciousness. However, a closely related defense mechanism, repression, is quite capable of permanently blocking out unpleasant aspects of reality.

Ruth, a twenty-eight-year-old woman who came to me for help with weight loss, clearly illustrates the power of repression. Approximately seventy-five pounds overweight, she was a walking encyclopedia of knowledge about diets and weight loss programs. She had tried them all. And the failure of each to help her solve her longstanding weight problem only served to heighten her feelings of low self-esteem and self-recrimination. It was in the course of exploring the reasons for her weight problem that Ruth's history of childhood sexual abuse first came to the surface.

When I first inquired about the possibility of sexual abuse, Ruth was adamant that nothing like that had ever happened to her. And she was not lying; she had no conscious memory of the abuse. However, as we continued to explore her childhood, the previously repressed memories of the abuse slowly began to surface.

The first thawing of repression appeared when one day she told me of a recent experience of agitation after listening to a lecture on the topic of childhood sexual abuse. She did not understand why she felt as she did and I did not share my suspicion. However, in the ensuing weeks she became more and more preoccupied with the question of whether she might have been abused as a child. She still had no memory of such an experience. But something within her would not let go of this nagging question. This was followed by further memories and much pain as the walls of repression quickly crumbled.

As we were later able to reconstruct her experience, it became clear that when Ruth was somewhere around seven years of age her father had sexually abused her on one or more occasions. The first feelings that came with this memory were those of deep shame and self-loathing. These feelings had never been far from Ruth, but prior to this memory she had tied them to her obesity. Repression had eliminated the memory of the abuse but had not completely eliminated the feelings of shame. These feelings were subsequently displaced onto her obesity, thus helping her to forget the sexual abuse.

As frequently happens when children have to deal

with trauma suffered at the hands of a parent, Ruth chose to be angry at herself rather than at her father. She felt she must have done something wrong, she must have been responsible for what her father had done to her. She felt herself to be disgusting and shameful. She felt that, at her core, she was a bad person.

Ruth began to gain weight soon after the experience of sexual abuse. In reconstructing this period of time she became aware of the fact that her weight gain was connected to a desire to hide her attractiveness from her father in an attempt to protect herself from further abuse. But it was also a way of making her body conform to how she felt inside. She felt ugly and concluded that she did not deserve an attractive body. Food thus became a form of self-abuse, a way of punishing herself. This continued for the twenty-one years between the abuse and when I first saw her, a neurotic self-abuse driven by guilt and shame over an experience Ruth did not even remember.

Repression may eliminate undesirable memories and experiences from consciousness, but it does so at a great price. Not only does it block growth by depriving the individual of the opportunity to face the conflictual feelings, but repression takes a good deal of psychic energy, leaving less energy available for other emotional commitments. The person who relies on repression is, therefore, often a depleted person who has little available to invest in others.

Rationalization

Rationalizations are excuses and explanations that superficially seem plausible but which actually distort and misrepresent reality. They are, in essence, a way of minimizing some unpleasant aspect of experience.

An example of rationalization is the person who, upon being fired from his job, responds by saying that it wasn't such a good job anyway and that he was planning to leave it as soon as he found another. Or someone might respond to an experience of rejection by a friend by saying, "Who cares! He wasn't much of a friend anyway." The responses to both these situations may contain an element of truth. The job may have been a bad one and the individual may have even been considering leaving it. Similarly, the friend may not have been a very good one. But in both situations these individuals are trying to make themselves feel better by means of a misrepresentation of their experience.

We frequently describe such uses of rationalization as the "sour grapes" tactic. This refers to a pretended disdain for something one cannot have, an allusion to Aesop's fable about the fox who, in an effort to save face, described as sour those grapes he could not reach. Sour grape reactions are rather thinly veiled attempts to disguise disappointment or hurt and are the most common form of rationalization used in dealing with emotional wounds.

Emotional Insulation

One final way in which we can eliminate emotional pain and yet avoid genuine healing of a wound is through the mental mechanism known as emotional insulation. Of the four defense mechanisms discussed, this is by far the most complex, and a number of distinct strategies of achieving such emotional insulation, while differing in some important ways, all serve the same general purpose of isolating an undesirable feeling and insulating this experience from consciousness.

In the most extreme form, multiple personalities are formed if the trauma is too extreme and other predisposing conditions are also present.[6] In such a situation, the main personality loses all memory of the trauma as well as all experience of the associated feelings. Both are split off into a dissociated part of personality, something psychopathologists call an alter personality. Each of these fragments of personality are isolated from the main personality and the emotions are managed by a strategy of "divide and conquer." If the strong emotions are kept isolated, they are then more easily contained. But this strategy of containment through isolation is seriously maladaptive and the splitting and isolation must be undone before healing can occur.

On a much less spectacular level, related mental processes are involved in the person who copes with a hurt by shutting down all emotions. Such a person (most often a male) eliminates the pain but also eliminates all other feeling states. We might describe him as emotionally insulated in that his emotions are put behind an impermeable wall and he lives out his life as if he had no emotions. Mr. Spock, the chief science officer of the USS *Enterprise* from the television series, "Star Trek," typifies such a person—overreliant on logic and rationality for solving all the problems of life. Emotions are not only alien to such a person, but are viewed as signs of weakness. While not all such persons are defending against hurt by such a process (some are merely imbalanced in their psychological development), such a posture does offer an excellent defense against feelings of hurt for many people. However, it is also equally effective in blocking growth because healing cannot occur until the hurts are faced head-on.

Summary

We began this chapter with the question of what exactly is involved in an experience of hurt. To briefly review what we have discovered, we could state that experiences of hurt are based on a perceived violation of trust. One of the first consequences of this is the experience of loss. In one way or another, emotional hurt is always experienced as the loss of something valuable. We feel ourselves to be alone, depleted, violated, damaged, or in some way less competent or capable of facing life. This sense of loss is usually accompanied by a feeling of sadness and vulnerability. This is the core of the pain we describe as hurt.

Vulnerability is usually covered over by anger very quickly. Anger serves to distract us from our pain by focusing our attention away from ourselves and onto the one whom we perceive as having been responsible for our hurt. It also serves to assuage our feelings of powerlessness. Usually the feelings of anger and pain will alternate, each serving as a defense against the other. We also noted that it is possible to get stuck in either of these phases of the hurt cycle and that the underlying pain and anger can be masked and presented in many disguised forms.

Finally, we explored the common expectation that time heals. What we discovered is that time is necessary but not sufficient for healing. To rely on time to heal is to rely on one of the mental mechanisms of defense to eliminate the feelings of pain, and this is much different than genuine healing.

This brings us to the next major section of the book, in which we will address the question of what emotional healing is and how we obtain it. What we will discover is that each of the components of personality involved in the emotional injury needs to be addressed in emotional healing, a process that will necessarily involve our emotions, our intellect, and our will. Anything less is insufficiently radical to address the deep and pervasive effects of significant emotional injury.

PART 2

The Context
of Emotional Healing

3

Reexperiencing the Pain

A wounded heart can with difficulty be healed.

—Goethe

Blessed are those who mourn for they shall be comforted.

—Jesus

The work of emotional healing involves three major tasks: reexperiencing the pain, reinterpreting the hurt, and releasing the anger. Many discussions of how to deal with hurt feelings tend to focus on only one of these three tasks, ignoring the others. But all three are essential if we are to experience genuine healing.

Each of the three major tasks addresses one principal sphere of personality and this is the reason that all three are essential. The first task, that of reconnecting with the pain of the emotional injury, is primarily an emotional one. This task is often experienced as the most difficult, but each is clearly difficult in its own way. The major difficulty of the emotional task is simply that of facing the pain that I have up to now worked so hard to avoid. This will be the focus of the present chapter.

The second task, that of reinterpreting the hurt, is primarily an intellectual one. This task is easily overlooked and is often not a part of discussions of emotional healing. However, many of the reasons people tend to get stuck in the third task, that of releasing their anger and forgiving the one who hurt them, have their roots in this second stage. The need to see the other person and the whole situation through new eyes is crucial if healing is to occur and this is the challenge of reinterpreting the hurt. The intellectual task will be the focus of chapter 4.

The final task, that of releasing the anger, is primarily a volitional one. Here we are called upon to exercise our will in doing something that is as difficult as anything a human being can be asked to do. Until we recognize how hard forgiveness really is, we fail to understand all that is involved with it. The volitional task will be the focus of chapter 5.

Genuine healing of damaged emotions involves, therefore, not just the emotions but also the intellect and the will. We must be careful not to interpret this model of healing in an overly mechanical fashion. In describing stages or tasks of healing, each of which addresses one primary sphere of personality, we are artificially separating things that in reality go together. Not only do the tasks tend to overlap, but to some extent each involves the spheres of personality that are dominant in another. Thus, for example, the first task clearly involves not just the emotions but both the will and the intellect as well. Facing head-on that which we did everything possible to avoid when we were first hurt is an act of great courage which requires real determination of will. But this stage of reexperiencing the hurt also involves the intellect in processing the emotions we encounter. The same is true of the other tasks. There is, therefore, no strict separation of the emotional, intellectual, and volitional aspects of the healing work even though each stage gives primacy to one of these spheres of functioning.

But all I have addressed so far is the *work* of healing. There is no denying the fact that emotional healing is hard work. But before we get into the details of this, we should pause to reflect on the *possibility* of healing.

Emotional Healing Is Possible

We need not be victims of our past! Although we often fail to recognize it as such, this is an essential part of the gospel. Unfortunately we too often spiritualize the gospel, seeing Christ's work of salvation merely in terms of forgiveness of our sins. But salvation is much more than this. Christ came to heal us of our wounds and to set us free from all that binds us. Hurts may be inevitable, but emotional healing is possible. Christ calls us to wholeness and makes this possible by his brokenness.

Too often people feel somewhat fatalistic about the damaging effects of emotional wounds. They may be bitter or depressed as a result of some hurt but feel, "I am what I am because of what has happened to me and there is nothing I can do about it now." Often they feel that the insights of depth psychology support this sort of attitude ("Wasn't it Freud who proved that if your mother weaned you too fast that you would be some kind of an emotional cripple for the rest of your life?"[1]). But this sort of fatalism is not a part of the major depth psychologies. Both psychology and Christianity affirm the possibility of our receiving healing of the emotional wounds of our past.

There is no question that we are influenced by our life experiences, and as we have already seen, these experiences inevitably involve hurt and emotional injury. But that is not the final word on the matter. Just because I may have been the victim of unfair treatment at the hands of others does not mean that I am doomed to struggle through life as an emotional cripple. Just because I have been hurt by others does not mean that I must continue in bondage to the pain and anger associated with those hurts. We need not be victims of our past.

The ancient Greek philosopher Epictetus noted that our experiences don't make us the people we are as much as our reactions to them. These reactions may be influenced by our experiences, but they are never determined by them. While caught up in the fury of the initial emotional response to a significant hurt, we may feel that we have no control whatsoever over our reactions. Anger and depression may seem to sweep over us like waves crashing over a sinking boat. At that early point in the experience of pain we may, in fact, not be able to do much more than hang on. But we can move beyond the controlling effects of such anger and pain. We can come to a point of being free to choose our reactions to the events of our past. Those reactions are not as determined as we feel them to be.

Alfred Adler, once a close associate of Sigmund Freud, described our experiences in life as providing the building blocks of our personality.[2] But a pile of building materials is not the same as a building. What remains is the task of the actual construction. The question is how we, the architects and builders, decide to arrange the building blocks in the construction of our lives. In other words, our past provides us with the raw materials of our personality but does not determine what we do with them.

Corrie ten Boom's experiences in the Nazi concentration camps of World War II taught her a similar lesson.

She reported that she came to understand that her captors could take her clothes and possessions, deprive her of food and medical care, torment her, and even kill her. But they could not determine how she would react to them. She did not have to hate. And by Christ's power, she did, in fact, experience healing of her hurts and overcame hatred with love and forgiveness. Healing of emotional wounds was possible for her and is also possible for us.

The tragedy is that many people continue to live in bondage to the past because they refuse to believe they can be set free from the tyrannizing effects of their hurts. Often they are not ready to forgive those who hurt them and so they cling to their anger and consequently also continue to embrace their pain. Or they may feel ready to forgive, and may have even tried to do so, but find themselves stuck in their anger and pain. Their efforts at forgiveness bring no relief, and they begin to lose hope that healing is possible.

Another group of people who live with long-term unhealed hurts appear to believe that healing may be possible but are simply afraid to try. Some may be afraid to ask for help. They may feel incapable of dealing with their hurts themselves but be too frightened to go to a pastor or therapist or to seek the help of a friend. Others may be afraid that they will take the necessary steps toward emotional healing only to find that such healing has still evaded them. Still others are simply afraid of experiencing more pain and, knowing that healing will involve pain, remain stuck in inertia and fear.

No Pain/No Gain

The notion that we have to experience more pain before we can be emotionally healed is quite unattractive to all but the most masochistic of us. Still our life experiences should certainly at least make this plausible. A personal incident may illustrate this. I recall a time when I broke my nose but put off going to a physician for several days. When I finally did get it x-rayed, I was advised that my nose would have to be rebroken in order to straighten it and remedy the breathing problems which were developing. Many people routinely avoid going to physicians and dentists for help out of the recognition that such help may involve more pain or discomfort. The obvious fact is that healing of our physical maladies often involves further pain.

In a similar way, emotional healing, if it is to be genuine and sufficiently radical to address the depths of our injury, will also inevitably involve pain. In emotional healing, this pain is not some new pain. Rather, it is a reexperiencing of the old pain which was caused by the original injury. As we observed in the last chapter, until this hurt is healed, it lives on within us, even if we are not conscious of it. In such a case, healing will necessarily involve bringing the hurt to the light of day and experiencing it again.

Quite often this means experiencing the pain with an intensity that we avoided when the hurt was initially encountered. The mechanisms of defense that we discussed in the last chapter all serve to short-circuit the pain, often eliminating it before it is really experienced. It is not, therefore, a matter of going over the same things again, but of experiencing the hurt in a different way from that which we allowed ourselves in the original situation. And then it is a matter of releasing this hurt.

The Role of Catharsis in Healing

An understanding of the principle of catharsis is important in appreciating why we must feel the hurt and not just try to cover it over. Coming from the Greek word meaning "purification," the concept of catharsis refers to a therapeutic release of pent-up emotions. The ancient Greeks used the term to describe the emotional purgation which spectators experience when viewing a tragic play. They judged this to be therapeutic, not simply entertaining. This use of drama in emotional healing is a clear forerunner of the contemporary practice of psychodrama, one of a number of psychotherapeutic procedures that capitalizes on catharsis.

The role of catharsis in modern psychology was first systematically studied by Joseph Breuer, a late nineteenth-century Viennese neurologist and colleague of Freud. Breuer became aware of the importance of catharsis when he noticed that hysterical symptoms (such as psychogenic paralysis or blindness) could be eliminated by having the person reexperience the feelings associated with the onset of these symptoms. Thus, for example, in his much-publicized treatment of a young woman named Anna O., Breuer reported that her mysterious and sudden onset of paralysis was totally eliminated by having her recall the events of the days immediately prior to the onset of the paralysis and release the feelings that were a part of those experiences.

Breuer's work with catharsis came to Freud's attention and together they continued to study its role in emotional healing. In *Studies in Hysteria*,[3] they presented the framework for what was to become the early psychoanalytic model of the mind, a model built around the central role of catharsis in healing. Within this model, the mind could be compared to a water balloon. If filled too full with water, the pressure will increase within the balloon until it either springs a leak or completely ruptures. Pressure, in this analogy, is comparable to the build-up of emotions and is experienced by a person as anxiety. The leak describes the role of other symptoms, either psychological or physiological, while the rupture refers to the more drastic experience of a psychotic break.

In this analogy, catharsis is the means of both preventing emotional problems and relieving any symptoms that may have begun to develop. Catharsis involves relieving the pressure on the system by draining off some of the built-up emotions. It is thus comparable to letting some of the water out of the balloon and thereby relieving the pressure and preventing rupture or distortion of its shape.

This rather hydraulic model of the mind has been much disputed since its earliest formulation, and even Freud himself later made substantial changes to it. Over time, he relied less and less on catharsis, coming to view it as secondary in importance to insight, a dimension of healing that we will discuss in the next chapter. However, other theorists continued to give catharsis a place of primacy, a place which it currently occupies in such approaches to psychotherapy as Gestalt therapy, primal therapy, bioenergetics analysis, and other expressive therapies.

Without going into the details of the ongoing debate surrounding the role of catharsis in psychotherapy,[4] most therapists would agree that catharsis is necessary but not sufficient for the healing of emotional wounds. It should be understood, therefore, that by placing this chapter on the emotional work of healing before the next two describing respectively the intellectual and volitional aspects of the process, I am not putting it in a position of primacy over the others. The emotional task is not more important, nor is it all-sufficient. But it is usually the first task encountered.

Mourning as the Core Emotional Task

The essence of the emotional work of healing is allowing ourselves to experience all the feelings associated with the hurt. As we noted in the previous chapter, at the basis of these feelings, and at the core of every emotional injury, is some experience of loss. Because of this, the mourning of losses is the core component of the emotional task.

Most of what we know about the process of mourning comes from the study of those who grieve the death of a loved one. However, much the same thing needs to occur in dealing with any loss. Like the formation of a scab on an open wound, mourning serves to start the process of repairing the psychological damage produced by the experience of hurt. Thus mourning is both healthy and necessary. In the absence of mourning, complete emotional healing is impossible.

In an important paper entitled "Mourning and Melancholia,"[5] Freud described the reactions to loss as dejection, detachment, and disinterest. He noted that when mourning a significant loss we tend to withdraw all emotional attachments and energy from the places where they were previously invested. In normal mourning, this process is temporary and is eventually followed by a reinvestment of emotional attachments.

Since the early work by Freud, a great deal of research has been done on mourning, much of it focusing on the stages involved in the grief process. This approach has been popularized by Elizabeth Kübler-Ross. Her book *On Death and Dying*[6] identifies five such stages—denial, anger, bargaining, depression, and acceptance. Less well known in popular circles, but more influential in professional ones, is the work of John Bowlby, who studied separations of children from their parents. Bowlby's research led him to identify three stages in what he called separation mourning—protest, despair, and detachment.[7] Subsequent studies by a large number of other researchers have identified a similar general pattern in a great variety of types of losses, the most commonly identified stages being numbness (primarily based on denial), emotional distress (primarily involving anger and depression), and recovery of emotional equilibrium (primarily identified by a readiness to move on with life and an ability to recall the past without being controlled by it).

It is important to note that, as with the tasks of healing, grieving of loss is hardly ever an orderly, sequential process. Seldom, if ever, are the stages neatly separated from each other. They may vary in order, length, and intensity, and may overlap, repeat themselves, or be skipped. In describing his own grief, C. S. Lewis says: "In grief, nothing 'stays put.' One keeps on emerging from a phase, but it always recurs. Round and round. Everything repeats. Am I going in circles, or dare I hope I am on a spiral? But if a spiral, am I going up or down?"[8] Furthermore, the course of mourning varies considerably from person to person, depending on several factors. The nature of the hurt, the psychological health of the person experiencing the hurt, and the adequacy of the support system of that individual all affect the process of mourning.

However, in spite of this variability, the broad contours of the three stages of numbness, emotional distress, and recovery of emotional equilibrium seem to be discernible. These stages were briefly described in chapter 2 during the discussion of our reaction to major trauma. There we noted that following such trauma it is normal for people to alternate between the emotional distress associated with reexperiencing the trauma and emotional numbness. After a while this is usually followed by a restabilization of functioning. Mourning of losses usually follows a similar set of stages.

Numbness is the result of denial and is usually the first reaction to the loss. We often describe such numbness as a state of shock. While it allows us to rally our psychological resources, it does not last long. As we noted in chapter 2, the reality of the loss usually breaks through this emotional insulation and leads to the experience of distress. The dominant feelings in this stage of emotional distress are anger and depression. The normal pattern is, then, to alternate between anger and depression as well as between emotional numbness and emotional distress. Finally, we speak of the restabilization of functioning occurring when the person is ready to resume life, able to recall the loss without being flooded with grief.

Grief Work

More important than noting the natural stages of the grief process is identifying what is necessary to ensure that we keep moving through these stages. Freud was the first to describe the active role we need to take in assisting the healing process and was the first to describe this activity as "grief work."

Grief work refers to the task of breaking through the denial and other defenses that separate me from my pain and allowing myself to experience and work through the feelings. In essence, it is allowing myself to mourn the losses which are at the core of my hurt.

The fact is that I have lost something as a result of the hurt. I must not seek to minimize this loss. Rather, I must allow myself to feel the sadness and anger appropriate to and associated with this loss. And I must allow myself to feel it over and over. The process takes time and can't be rushed or regulated. But if I face the feelings head-on, I will then be able to face the subsequent intellectual and volitional tasks and I will move toward healing.

Some people seem to do grief work quite naturally and may not be consciously aware of having to apply effort to the task. (They will, however, certainly be aware of the pain involved in the mourning and in that sense are aware of the difficulty of the task.) For others, this work seems unnatural and everything within them seeks to avoid it. If they do manage to avoid it, they may eventually move beyond the feelings of loss but will have failed to resolve the grief or heal the hurt associated with it. If they stick with the feelings, however, they will make progress.

Mourning as Reparative

Mourning is sometimes described as a reparative response to hurt. This means that it fosters healing. In contrast, ways of distancing ourselves from pain serve to retard healing. Mourning can thus be thought of as a way in which we actively work toward the repair of the emotional damage done by the hurt.

Folk psychology seems to correctly recognize this concept. Most people are prepared to acknowledge that, at least for others, crying after a significant loss is not only appropriate but helpful. Obviously there is some sex stereotyping involved in this issue, the common stereotype being that while women may need such a release, men often do not. But men who judge themselves not to need such emotional release usually still conclude that most other men do. In other words, they correctly recognize the general principle and err only in the conclusion that they are somehow different enough from the rest of humanity to be outside this otherwise general law of human nature.

It does, however, seem to be a general law of therapeutic psychology that crying and other forms of emotional release are healing. They are seldom all that is necessary for the healing of significant hurts, but they are an essential part of the process.

Another example of a reparative response to the experience of emotional pain is talking about the hurt. You may have noticed that someone who has just suffered some major emotional injury often shows a great need to talk about the experience, repeating the details over and over. This is quite demanding on friends and family, but it is essential that the grieving person talk things through in this manner. Talking, in such situations, is like crying. It reflects the grief work of emotional reexperiencing and is a reparative activity.

Nonreparative responses to emotional wounds are those which block our experience of the emotions. The defense mechanisms described in the preceding chapter are the most commonly employed nonreparative responses, but these are all unconscious. In addition, we also consciously try to get our minds off our pain. We may need to do this on occasion in order to continue to function, but we should always view such coping strategies as temporary.

This is the crucial difference between coping with our pain and defending against it. Those things that we do to cope with our suffering do not eliminate the pain but rather help us continue to function in the midst of it. Defense mechanisms, on the other hand, are designed to eliminate pain. Being with friends, using spiritual resources such as prayer, meditation, and Bible reading, even temporarily losing ourselves in our work, a good book, or some form of entertainment, all can be valuable aids to our coping. The danger comes, however, in using any of these as more permanent ways of avoiding the pain.

When attempting to distance oneself from the pain, it is important to take care lest you get so far from it that you forget that it is still there. Unless you absolutely must, make sure you never completely shut the door to the mental room that contains the pain. Try to leave it open at least a crack so you do not forget the important work that must still be done in that room and so you can get back into it as easily as possible. If the door is shut and sealed so securely that the pain is eliminated, defense mechanisms have replaced coping strategies and healing is now more remote.

On the other hand, once genuine healing has occurred, there is no need to seal the door shut. After emotional wounds are healed they are not forgotten. In fact, one criterion of genuine healing is the ability to remember the traumatic or hurtful incident fully. But it is now remembered without the acute pain. It is memory without the sting.

A Case Illustration

To illustrate how this reparative reexperiencing of the emotional wound actually works, let us return to the case of Ruth, the victim of childhood sexual abuse described in the previous chapter. Recall that initially Ruth had no memory of the abuse. What she faced was the residue left over after repression had eliminated both recall of the trauma and most of the emotions associated with it, namely, her struggle with overeating and her feelings of low self-esteem.

Deep feelings of shame and self-loathing were Ruth's first emotional response to recovering the memory of her experience of sexual abuse. She had never been a stranger to bad feelings about herself, but these were suddenly much more intense than she had ever previously experienced. She took upon herself the shame of the sexual abuse and felt herself to be disgusting. No words on my part seemed able to help her see that as a little girl of seven she was not in any way responsible for what happened. Her first experience of the pain from the abuse was anger, but this anger was turned back upon herself.

After several weeks of ever-deepening spirals of self-loathing, I pointed out to her that she seemed to prefer to be angry at herself rather than experience her anger at her father. This interpretation served its intended purpose and gave her permission to gradually begin to experience her rage at him. But it remained a difficult task for her to keep in touch with these feelings. She found innumerable creative ways of avoiding her anger at him. She felt guilty for her hatred of her father and quickly, by this strategy, again shifted the focus off her anger and off him. This was followed by a summary and premature attempt to forgive him. Ruth reported to me one day that her anger was all behind her now that she had been able to forgive him. But this ritualistic act served as no more than another temporary diversion, and the feelings of anger welled up again within a day or so.

A turning point came when Ruth saw that her feelings did not demand any particular action on her part in relation to her father. She realized that her fear of feeling was a fear of action, that is, a fear of having to confront her father. She concluded that this would never be possible and, even if it were, that it was not a course of action she was willing to consider. I encouraged her to ignore that question, telling her that even if her father was dead and a direct confrontation with him quite impossible, she would still have to face her feelings if she was to ever be emotionally free and whole. This understanding gave her the courage to take the next step toward her feelings, one that opened the flood gates quite rapidly.

Almost immediately Ruth began to experience waves of deep hatred and rage toward her father. Within the safety of my office, she felt free to allow these to pour out, session after session. She also began to write letters to her father, letters which I encouraged but which I told her were never to be sent. This again gave her the courage to feel her feelings more deeply and to begin to work them through in relation to him. These letters, and her exploration of her feelings, were very difficult for her. In fact, she described it as the most difficult thing she had ever done in her life.

One of the reasons this exploration of her feelings of anger was so difficult was that Ruth repeatedly and quite automatically moved back from the feelings of anger to those of hurt. Her sense of woundedness was deep and she vacillated between feeling angry and sad. Her sadness was a deep despair focused on the notion that she had lost something that she could never recover. She felt damaged and defective. As a result, she felt worthless and shameful.

And so she would spend a session or two on her anger and then a session or two on what an awful person she was and how damaged and defective she was. This rapid alternation of focus was itself a defense, and I pointed this out to her, encouraging her to choose one side and see if she could stay with those feelings longer.

At this stage we moved into an exploration of her feelings of loss. What she discovered was that as a result of the abuse she felt a loss of value, a loss of purity, and a loss of wholeness. She felt cheap, dirty, and broken. With these feelings came a resurgence of depression, but this time her depression wasn't simply a turning of her anger back upon herself. This time it was much more a mourning of her losses. She began to mourn the loss of her father, a father whom she had idealized as a little girl and even, to some extent, during the years since the abuse. She had tried to maintain the illusion of respect for him by turning her anger upon herself and her sadness now was her response to the loss of this illusion and the loss of the father she had always wanted.

She also became aware that the experience of abuse had resulted in a loss of innocence which she deeply grieved. She felt that childhood itself had been ripped from her and that she was suddenly thrust into adulthood. During this stage of therapy she wrote a poem entitled "The Loss of Innocence," and this was a most helpful part of her mourning.

Slowly and systematically it was necessary for Ruth to experience each of the major emotions that had been stirred up by the trauma of the abuse. The anger and the pain were the dominant ones, but in her case she also had to explore and reexperience the feelings of shame and guilt. Each of these needed to be expressed. It would not have been enough for her merely to reexperience these feelings but hold them all inside. The pain had to be expressed. This is the principle of catharsis and was the first step toward healing.

Sharing the Pain

One question that we need to consider at this point is whether it is necessary to share the feelings of hurt with someone else. Ruth had to do so because, as is usually the case in adults who have experienced childhood sexual abuse, her feelings were so repressed and complicated that professional help was necessary. But what about less traumatic experiences of hurt? Can't we just work through them ourselves? Is there a need to share them with anyone else?

I believe that hurts are best healed by sharing the feelings of the experiences with someone else. Humans are made in such a way that experiences cry out to be shared. Think about the experience of a beautiful sunset. Something within most of us desires the presence of someone with whom we can share such an experience. If no one can experience it firsthand with us, we long to tell someone about it. This reflects the deep and fundamental social nature of humans. We were created for relationships, and it is in these relationships that we fully experience both the pleasures of life and the healing of our wounds.

This need to share an experience with others is the reason why many otherwise successful criminals are caught. What satisfaction is there in committing the perfect crime and not being able to tell anyone about it? Even quite routine and far less than perfect crimes such as simple tax evasion are often detected after people share their accomplishments with friends who then tell someone else, until someone finally tells the authorities.

Although the experience of hurt may make us want to retreat from others and curl up in some hidden cave in the back of our psyche, at the same time something in us cries out for love. Unless we have been repeatedly hurt and never yet able to experience any healing of these wounds, this longing for nurturance and succor seems to be a usual accompaniment of hurt. We seem to need to share such experiences. And we need the care, support, and love that we can receive only from another person.

But there is another reason why the experience of the hurt needs to be shared for it to be healed. Hurts are interpersonal in nature and the instrument of healing must match the instrument of affliction. We were hurt by a person and it is, therefore, in a personal relationship that our healing can be best effected. The hurt begins to be healed as the pain is shared with someone who accepts me and is willing to listen to and accept my expression of hurt and anger.

Bear One Another's Burdens

In a remarkable way, sharing an experience does make the load less heavy. The biblical injunction to bear one another's burdens (Gal. 6:2) rests on the obvious fact that shared loads are lighter. To share an experience of pain with someone who is willing to listen empathically is to allow them to take our burden upon themselves and thereby share it with us. And in sharing, our load is lightened and we are strengthened.

This is really the core of what professional helpers do in counseling and psychotherapy. More than this is involved, but it is my conviction that the essential curative core of the relationship is one person sharing his or her pain, struggles, and confusion with another who takes the pain upon him- or herself and thereby shares the load.[9] Healing relationships of any sort are always built around this essential core.

Christ himself is described as bearing our burdens, carrying our sorrows, taking upon himself our sickness and infirmities, and thereby healing us (Isa. 53:4; Matt. 8:17). God's solution to the human problem (sin and its resulting alienation from self, others, the world, and God) was immensely personal. He sent his Son to become a human and to take the sin and sickness of the human race upon himself. By his death, we live. By his brokenness, we are made whole. By his wounds, we are healed.

Because Jesus came to us and suffered with and for us, he understands our suffering and is able to share our burdens. This is his great qualification as our helper when we hurt and need to share our experience with someone. Thus, when we feel ourselves overwhelmed by our hurts, disappointments, or losses, we should remember that Jesus is always available to share these burdens with us. The psalms give many rich examples of people pouring out their pain, anger, doubt, confusion, and hurt to God. God's unconditional acceptance of his children in and through Christ means that he accepts us with whatever struggles we bring to him. By sharing them with him, we are able to experience and explore things which are often otherwise unbearable.

But sharing experiences with God should not replace sharing them with other humans. God made us in such a way that our needs are not met solely by being in relationship with him. Adam had a perfect unbroken relationship with God. Genesis records that Adam and God regularly walked together in the garden of Eden and used such times to talk with each other. And yet, in spite of this incredible degree of intimate communion, God declared that it was not good that Adam was alone! His human nature demanded communion with other humans. He needed to share with another human and not merely with God. And so it is with us.

Sometimes sharing feelings with God is a way to prepare for sharing them with others. At other times, problems seem more readily shared with other humans and God's love, in these situations, is communicated to us through the love of another person. Concluding that certain hurts cannot be shared as meaningfully with God as with another person is not an indication of a lack of spirituality on my part. Sometimes I may need a listener with a face that I can see or arms with which I can be hugged. On the other hand, sometimes my hurts can be uniquely borne by Christ, who has suffered in all ways in which I could ever suffer and whom I can therefore meet quite uniquely in my own suffering.

The Need for Confrontation

One final matter which requires consideration is the question of whether we have to confront the one who hurt us in order to experience full healing. In spite of the fact that some authors view such confrontation as indispensable for healing,[10] it is my experience that it is neither always necessary nor even always desirable. When it is either necessary or desirable, it most frequently requires much preparation and is seldom the relationship of sharing that helps one take the first steps toward healing.

The fact that such confrontation is not necessary is made clear by the observation that people are able to resolve hurts inflicted upon them by people who are dead by the time they are ready to face the feelings. And for this we can thank God. It would be an awfully cruel world if I could not only be hurt by people, but the healing of my wounds depended upon their availability to me when I was ready for healing. This is not the case, however, and the testimony of many who have been able to forgive and move beyond the hurts brought upon them by people they now have no way of contacting should answer this question definitively.

It is difficult to state in the abstract when it is necessary to confront the person who hurt me. In general, it is something that should be deferred until I am absolutely ready for such action. I need to be sure of my motives for wanting to talk with the other about my hurt and I need time to prepare for such action. This preparation is something that often requires the help of another. In other words, confronting the person who hurt me does not usually replace the need for sharing the feelings with someone. The reason for this is simple. Confrontation done apart from such preparatory work is usually little more than catharsis for my anger. But, as we have seen, this is only one part of the emotional picture that needs to be explored. The person who hurt me is seldom the one best able to help me work through all these feelings.

Hurts incurred in marriages or comparably intimate and committed relationships are sometimes an exception to this rule, but much still depends on the nature of the hurt as well as the nature of the relationship. In a healthy marriage where both partners have learned to keep short emotional accounts and deal with things as they come up, it is often possible to go straight to one's spouse with a hurt experienced in this relationship and deal with it directly. But the more time that has passed since the hurt and the greater the number of past hurts which have not yet been resolved, the more likely it is that the person will need help from someone else in preparing to deal with these feelings.

Once I have my feelings somewhat straightened out for myself, a direct encounter with the person who hurt me is often appropriate. If I continue to be in regular contact with this person (particularly spouses and family members), such a confrontation is essential. However, there is generally less need to confront someone from my past with whom I have no present contact. I usually won't know how I will need to deal with the other person until I first deal with the feelings in myself. Then, and only then, will I be in a position to respond to the other person as separate from myself and my hurt. I am also then in a better position to share my feelings and not be dependent upon any given response on his or her part.

I usually judge readiness for such an encounter by the criterion of whether I can feel content with the encounter regardless of how the other person responds. If I need the other to apologize, ask my forgiveness, or offer any comparable response of contrition, I am usually not yet sufficiently ready to deal with them.

The best reason for dealing directly with the person who hurt me is to restore a relationship. But of course it

takes the willingness of both parties for such an outcome, and even then it is far from guaranteed. So I can't
go to people who have hurt me and restore the relationship. All I can do is share my feelings with them, letting
them know how they hurt me and where I am in the
process of forgiving them, and hope that this may clear
the way for a restoration of the relationship. If they
receive what I give them, we may be reconciled. If not,
at least I have communicated my hurt and my desire to
forgive them.

I realize that others will give different answers to this
question and it is a matter of a sufficiently personal
nature that people need to decide for themselves what
they are called to do in any given situation. No one
should tell you not to talk directly with the person who
hurt you. All anyone has the right to do is to challenge
you to examine your motives and your readiness for
such action. Similarly, no one should tell you that you
must deal directly with the other person. The most that
should be done in this regard is to encourage you to consider whether such action would be appropriate. Beyond
this, I would suggest that dogmatic answers to the question be avoided.

Summary

The focus of this chapter has been the first step in
emotional healing, the emotional task of reexperiencing
our hurts. I have spoken of reexperiencing the hurt,
assuming that since the occasion of the hurtful experience we have begun to gain some distance from the feelings. Obviously, however, this has implications for what
we should do if we find ourselves in the midst of some
present hurt. The implication of what we have explored
in this chapter is that I should not seek to avoid the feelings associated with the hurt but should rather let

myself experience them and work them through while they are still alive. Doing so before they are repressed or in some other way buried makes the healing process much easier.

To do this requires that I have sufficient emotional support available from others to allow me to stay in touch with my feelings of pain or anger. It also means that I must not just feel these feelings, but I must also share them with others. If I do this, I should be able to move to the next stage, reinterpreting the experience, all the sooner. The good news which we identified in this chapter is that even old hurts can be healed once I am ready to begin by reexperiencing the feelings.

Learning to keep short accounts with our feelings is the main way we can contribute to our own emotional healing. Dealing with feelings, rather than ignoring them, allows us to keep hurts and their emotional consequences from compounding. We may not be able to prevent future experiences of hurt, but what we can do is deal with them when they happen rather than follow what is almost a knee-jerk reaction for most of us—avoiding the pain and getting rid of the negative emotions in any way possible. Understanding the process of recovering old hurts should, therefore, encourage us to keep our emotional accounts current.

4

Reinterpreting the Hurt

But there is no veil like light and no adamantine armor against hurt like the truth.

—George MacDonald

The truth shall set you free.

—Jesus

While it is stating the obvious to indicate that emotional healing necessarily involves our feelings, it is much easier to fail to recognize the fact that such healing must of the same necessity involve our intellect. This is without question the most frequently overlooked and least understood component of the healing process.

Those who use their intellect in dealing with emotional hurts often use it in a counterproductive way. Rationalization was described in chapter 2 as a defense mechanism that has at its core a misuse of thinking. In it, thinking is used to distort reality and thus to minimize pain. Tragically, our intellect is all too often a part of such defensive, reality-distorting strategies for dealing with pain and unpleasant experiences. As noted in chapter 2, such uses of thinking actually impair healing.

This perversion of thinking is one of the consequences of sin. The human capacity for thought—designed by God to be something that helps us appreciate the world he gave us, accomplish the tasks he set before us, and cope with the problems and hurts we experience in doing so—is distorted through sin in such a way that it often becomes part of the problem rather than part of the solution. Our intellect must be involved in the healing process, but in order for it to be part of the solution, it must play a reality-affirming role.

Truth and Psychospiritual Well-Being

The intellectual activity that is necessary for healing is that which brings truth to bear on the situation. In order to effectively deal with emotional wounds we must correctly understand the whole experience of our hurt. Our damaged emotions tend to distort how we perceive both the one who hurt us and ourselves. In our woundedness, our perceptions are shaped by our feelings. For healing to occur, our perceptions must be brought into line with reality, with truth. Truth, like light, allows us to clearly perceive reality. Then, and only then, is healing possible.

When Jesus stated that it is through knowing the truth that we are set free, he was not merely talking about the role of understanding or reality affirmation in emotional healing. The truth he referred to was himself and the healing he described was the comprehensive healing of our beings that is intended through salvation. Jesus is Truth and knowing him does set us free. This is the essence of the gospel. True freedom comes only from knowing the source of all truth, Jesus Christ.

But this passage communicates to us because we already know the reference point for this revelation of the character of Jesus—that truth does set one free. We sometimes feel that we can be free of the unpleasant aspects of our life situation by escaping into fantasy or illusion. We pretend things are not as they are and hope that our pretending will make it real, but it doesn't. Illusions do not provide freedom. Rather, they produce bondage. The great tragedy of our attempts to escape from reality is that so often we are successful. But our escape is from the frying pan to the fire. What we get is not freedom but illusion. True freedom comes when we see the illusions and lies of our life for what they are. This crucial function of truth in achieving and maintaining psychological well-being has received emphasis in a great variety of systems of therapeutic psychology and has become a cornerstone of sound psychotherapeutic practice.

William Glasser, best-known for his development of reality therapy,[1] noted that the one thing persons suffering from mental illnesses all share in common is their avoidance of truth. In one way or another, they all distort reality. They seek to avoid accepting things as they are and attempt, by means of various mental mechanisms, to distort reality. They are all in bondage to illusions of one form or another. A person suffering from schizophrenia may mask his feelings of impotence with delusions of grandeur, while someone experiencing a serious obsessive-compulsive disorder may engage in ritualistic hand washing many times a day as a way of warding off feelings of shame or guilt. What such people need, according to Glasser, is to face reality, to face the truth. This truth will not, as they fear, destroy them. Rather, it will liberate them. This ability to accept reality is, in Glasser's view, the major hallmark of mental health and it is the route to health for those who face psychological problems of any sort.

Rational-emotive therapy, developed in the 1950s by Albert Ellis, also gives the liberating role of truth great emphasis. The assumption of this approach is that irrational beliefs underlie all psychological problems. Irrational beliefs are, among other things, those that are not based on objective consensual reality.[2] In short, they are beliefs which are not true. Thus, for example, if I believe that everyone must like me if I am to be able to feel that I have worth, then I am operating within an understanding of reality that is erroneous. And I will experience psychological problems because of this lack of contact with reality. Christian versions of this sort of cognitive approach to therapy replace irrationality with the notion of holding unbiblical convictions, but the basic view is similar.[3] When I believe and live according to convictions which are untrue, I cannot expect to be emotionally or spiritually whole. Living in the light of beliefs and perceptions that are true to reality is the key to emotional well-being and the route to emotional healing.

Freud also recognized the essential liberating value of truth. Noting that we often live with a very distorted view of present reality, he suggested that such avoidance of truth is based in both our tendency to defend against conflict and emotional pain and in developmental arrests. The mechanisms of defense, discussed in chapter 2, are blatant attempts to change reality because it is unpleasant, but our distortion of truth is even deeper. We often look at the world through the eyes of a little boy or girl, having failed to allow our expectations of others and our view of ourself and others to grow up. These fixations in our development also produce a distortion of reality, and they need to be overcome for emotional healing and psychological well-being. Truth, for Freud, was reality. Knowing the truth about ourselves requires, according to Freud, facing ourselves as we really are.

If, for example, a young boy experienced repeated childhood hurt at the hands of a highly critical father whom he could never please, it would be quite understandable that as an adult he might have trouble relating to men in positions of authority over him. He might, for example, tend to view them as dangerous and have difficulty letting down his guard in such relationships. Or he might get caught up in trying to win the approval of male authority figures, desperately trying to get from them what he never got from his father.

While such feelings may be understandable, they nonetheless involve clear distortions of reality. Such a person sees the world, particularly his relationships with authority figures, through the eyes of the little boy who lives on within him. His judgment that all men are demanding and critical is an overgeneralization that needs correction. And the best way to correct it, according to Freud, is to understand its source. Bringing this to consciousness sheds light on the situation and begins to bring freedom. The monsters we fear in the dark closets of our unconscious mind always shrink in size when we turn the light of truth upon them.

This is the heart of the psychoanalytic view of the therapeutic nature of insight. As understood in psychoanalysis, insight could be described as a knowledge of our own conscious and unconscious feelings and thoughts that constructively alters our perception of ourselves and of others, bringing both into greater conformity with reality.[4] Therapeutic insight does not merely refer to the acquisition of some piece of information about myself. It is a connection between my inner and outer worlds, between my past and my present, between my unconscious and my conscious states of mind. And genuine insight, as opposed to mere knowledge, always promotes healing and growth.

Although Carl Jung did not use the language of truth, he also had a view of growth and healing that makes important use of the concept. The crucial truths about ourselves that we require for psychological health are, Jung believed, primarily contained in that aspect of the unconscious he called the shadow. The shadow refers to that part of personality which has been repressed because it does not seem to fit well with our ego ideal. In other words, it is everything about ourselves which is true but which we seek to avoid facing.

Our shadow is like an alter ego. We cannot run away from it. It is always with us. We can ignore it but only to our own detriment. If we fail to take it into account when we consider who we are, we misperceive ourselves. If, however, we face the truth about ourselves, we become more whole. We are also more capable of changing ourselves once we accept who we are. Changes of self-image based on denial and repression are not real self-change at all.

Only when we truly accept ourselves as we are, shadow and all, will we be able to begin working toward constructively changing ourselves. Seeing ourselves as we really are, that is, accepting the truth about ourselves, is the basis of all genuine human growth.

A Case Illustration

In order to see how the truth does indeed set us free, let us return to the discussion of Ruth, the woman struggling with the consequences of childhood sexual abuse. In the previous chapter we explored the emotional work that was necessary as the first stage of Ruth's healing. But a reinterpretation of her hurt in which truth was brought to bear on her experience was also an essential part of the healing process. The first step in this new understanding of the hurt was the act of remembering.

Freud noted that traumas which are repressed will inevitably be repeated until they are remembered. Repetition replaces recall. He called this phenomenon the repetition compulsion, describing it as the almost irresistible impulse to repeat repressed hurtful experiences regardless of the pain they produce.[5] In Ruth's case this had taken the form of continuing to get caught in abusive, self-defeating relationships with men. None of these relationships had involved actual physical abuse. However, most had involved emotional abuse, and all had been frustrating and hurtful.

For reasons that she did not understand, Ruth felt strangely attracted to males who were hostile and emotionally insensitive and who, in many ways, were losers. In spite of the fact that she was quite intelligent and was a university graduate, most of her dating had been with men who were high school dropouts. Several of these had been alcoholics or drug abusers, one was repeatedly in trouble with the law, and none had been in any way people whom she would want to marry. When I drew this pattern to her attention, she told me that she didn't deserve a better man. She also felt that men who were more desirable would not be attracted to her. But these were no more than rationalizations for behavior that she herself did not understand.

The memories of the abuse began to bring understanding and emotional freedom in her relationships with men. This did not come immediately, but over time Ruth came to understand the link between the hurts she had experienced from her father and the pattern of her heterosexual relationships. She began to understand the irrationality of this pattern. She was, in many ways, picking men who would be emotionally cruel and abusive in order to punish herself for what she felt to have been her responsibility in her childhood sexual experiences. With this understanding, she began to alter her behavior and move into more satisfying relationships with men. Recall slowly replaced repetition and began to bring freedom.

As Ruth began to remember the experience of sexual abuse, she was initially afraid that she would not be able to handle what she was encountering. She feared the strength of her emotions. This was her monster in the dark. But bringing the monster out into the light of day reduced it down to size. She was quite capable of dealing with the strength of her feelings. In fact, she began to feel stronger and less frightened as soon as the memories were recovered from unconsciousness. Her monster turned out to not be as bad as she had feared, and this is the experience of most people. She was empowered by remembering because she was recovering a lost part of herself. While we often want to cut off such weak or hurt parts of ourselves, to do so always impairs us much more than living in a way that fully embraces all aspects of who we are. Accepting the hurt and damaged parts of herself immediately made Ruth more whole.

Another important way in which Ruth had lost a part of herself was through her denial of her dependency longings. She had not only denied and repressed the memory of the abuse and much of the pain associated with it, she also had attempted to eliminate the longings for intimacy that had been associated with the hurt because they were very much a part of her relationship with her father. Consequently she had come to feel that she did not need men in the way other women did. She tried to be strong, independent, and autonomous, and avoided at all costs experiencing or expressing any needs, particularly needs for intimacy and dependence on others. But this did not eliminate such needs. Rather, it just further fractured her personality, these dependency longings being relegated to some hidden corner of her personality.

In a manner very much akin to what Jung described as the reconciliation to one's shadow, Ruth slowly came to see that her need for dependency was not the source of danger that she had judged it to be and could be accepted as a part of herself. She did not need to purge herself of this need, and, in fact, she was unable to do so. But she could reown these parts of herself and thereby move toward wholeness. And this is what she did. In the light of these insights she acknowledged how much she still longed for an emotionally intimate relationship with a male and subsequently took the first steps toward such relationships.

Through all of this work, Ruth was using her intellect as a resource for healing. She was remembering, analyzing, and reinterpreting her experience. We could say she was thinking her way through her hurt. But it was thinking that was not divorced from feeling, and this is the big difference between the work of healing and the efforts of defense. Thinking and feeling are inextricably linked. Efforts to divorce them are destructive of emotional well-being while efforts to relate them are health-enhancing. This is why we must be careful to recognize that emotional work can never be separated from intellectual work.

Construals Shape Reactions

How we understand an experience clearly shapes how we respond to it. For example, if my boss calls me to his office, I will react with eager anticipation if I infer a connection between my recent success in some assignment that he gave me and the present call. If, on the other hand, I construe the contact as a likely reprimand for my recent slothful performance, I will not approach the meeting with the same anticipation. In this regard you may note that you sometimes struggle to know how to interpret an experience in order to know how you should feel about it. I recall recently trying to understand a somewhat ambiguous encounter with an acquaintance which could have been interpreted either as an insult or a compliment. My feelings about this encounter were dependent upon how I understood it. I first had to decide how to interpret the experience before I could feel the feelings that would be associated with that construal.

Experiences of hurt are often easily misconstrued because of the intense emotions involved. In such a situation we frequently have a distorted recall of what actually occurred. We may remember things being said that were not said, and we may similarly have a distorted recall of behavior. Our memory gets processed through our hurt emotions and is easily shaped to fit those emotions.

Because of the way in which memory easily gets distorted by feelings, marital therapists often find it quite instructive to videotape fights between couples they are trying to help and then replay these encounters to the couple. This is a dramatic way of helping them become aware of how distorted their perceptions of their interactions are. Such misperceptions need to be corrected before the emotional wounds can be healed.

Karen and Wayne, the couple we discussed in chapter 1, very much needed such correction of misperceptions and misconstruals before they could experience healing of the hurts encountered in their troubled relationship. Both Karen and Wayne felt their trust to have been seriously violated by the other. The core of these perceived violations of trust lay, for each of them, in the perception that the other had implicitly promised to meet needs in the way they each had observed their respective parents meeting each other's needs. Since they came from different families, however, this expectation was doomed to produce frustration and disappointment.

My sessions with this couple initially took the form of reviewing their week in order to identify and rectify misunderstandings or other communication problems which had occurred. The problem was that it was almost impossible to get them to agree on exactly what it was that had actually happened. They remembered each other saying and doing things different from what the other was prepared to acknowledge.

With this observation I shifted tactics and began to stop them in the midst of a transaction in the office with me and ask them each to tell me what they had just seen or heard the other say. Through this, I, as a somewhat objective observer, could bring a degree of reality to bear on their distorted perceptions and slowly they began to form construals of what was taking place between them that were better representations of what was actually occurring.

These people were not stupid. Their misperceptions were not based on a lack of intelligence. Rather, they were thinking through their hurt emotions. They were hearing only what they wanted to hear, confirming assumptions about how little the other cared and how insensitive the other was.

Accurate listening requires that these damaged emotions be dealt with directly (in the manner described in the previous chapter) and that we begin to get beyond hearing through our past hurts and pain. This sort of careful listening, combined with actively asking myself whether what I *think* I heard is actually what was spoken or intended, is a demanding task that requires a great deal of motivation and the use of critical intellectual skills.

One of the most important ways in which experiences of hurt tend to be misconstrued is in our perception of the person who hurt us. As we experience the painful feelings associated with the emotional injury, we usually begin to view the other person in quite distorted ways, and these distorted perceptions block our healing. For such healing we must, therefore, reinterpret the experience of hurt and bring our perceptions of the other person into closer contact with reality.

Seeing the Other as "Like Me"

In the midst of my experience of hurt it is inevitable that I will come to view the one I consider to be responsible for my pain as some kind of a villain or monster. Everything I know gets interpreted through the experience of my hurt, and his behavior in the situation that produced my hurt becomes the key to understanding what I judge to be that individual's essential nature.

The problem with such a perception is that it is almost always a *mis*perception. I am usually wrong in equating people with any one aspect of their behavior. Even in attempting to interpret what I may perceive to be a more general pattern of behavior, I am almost certain to misunderstand people's motivations and character when I view them through the lens of my hurt. But perhaps the most crucial element in such a misperception is the notion that the other person is quite unlike me and I am quite unlike him. Suddenly the world is divided into two groups—villains and victims. Along with others who hurt me in past situations, the one who is responsible for my present hurt is in the former category, while others with whom I identify in their present or past hurt stand with me in the latter category.

We seem to take some comfort in this categorization. In fact, it is quite a seductive form of comfort and often very difficult to either resist or relinquish. We speak of people going through life playing a victim role, asking others by means of their behavior to punish them or take advantage of them and thus to confirm their construal of themselves and the world. Self-pity becomes the reward for such an unfortunate lot in life. Although such people complain about the cards they have been dealt in the game of life, they are quite unwilling to stop playing the particular game they are playing and relinquish the victim role. The payoffs for this role are too great for them to be willing to give it up.

Seeing the one who hurt me as more like than unlike me is the first step in cutting through this sort of erroneous construal of the context of my hurt. This involves seeing the other person as being, like me, weak and needy. In his book *Forgive and Forget*, Lewis Smedes describes this as requiring the gift of new eyes, a kind of magic eyes that allow me to see past behavior to needs.[6] It involves seeing others as I see myself and consequently seeing them as like me.

One important part of this new perception is seeing that those who hurt me more likely than not did so while coping with personal hurts, needs, and feelings of inadequacy. This does not excuse people for what they did. In fact, it is precisely because what they did is inexcusable that forgiveness is necessary. But when I am able to understand that the actions which hurt me arose out of other people's misguided ways of dealing with their own limitations and wounds, I am then on my way to becoming ready to forgive them for what they did.

Something begins to change when I begin to see the one who hurt me as being like me. The compartmentalization of the world into villains and victims begins to dissolve and my hurt almost immediately begins to take on a different demeanor. Many people describe this as an "ah-ha" experience wherein, like any genuine insight, things can never look quite the same again. In allowing myself to experience this insight I take an enormous step—for the first time since the experience of hurt, I allow myself to identify with the one who hurt me. And until I do this, I cannot be healed of the hurt.

In the light of this we must recognize that seeing the other as a villain and myself as a victim is a defensive posture, not a healing one. It is a way of dealing with the pain, but it is not one that genuinely helps me experience healing. It is a way of nursing the hurt and nurturing myself through self-pity, something that may be necessary as a first response to the hurt but which must be ultimately relinquished if I am to experience real emotional healing.

Seeing Myself as "Like the Other"

A related aspect of this work of reinterpreting the experience of hurt is to see myself as more like than unlike the person who hurt me. The previous task involved altering my perception of the other person. This task involves altering my perception of myself and it further prepares me to begin to identify with the one who hurt me.

In this task my attention shifts from the other back to myself. In reality, I move back and forth between these two foci frequently in this process of reinterpreting the hurt. But as my attention focuses on myself, part of the necessary reinterpretation involves a recognition that I am also one who has hurt and continues to hurt others. I hurt them in the same way in which I was hurt—by acting out of my own needs and brokenness and, in so doing, being insensitive to the needs of others.

Reflection on a given incident where I know I was the cause of the hurt of another is a very useful exercise in this regard. We may never have done this carefully before. We may have been too quick to excuse ourselves or we may have blamed the taking of hurt on the other whom we may have perceived as being overly thin-skinned. But there is great potential for growth in examining the matter more closely. How exactly did I hurt the other and why did I behave in the manner in which I did? Usually, when asking this sort of question, I will be able to see that it wasn't willful malice on my part that caused the hurt. Much more frequently I was too busy coping with my own inadequacies and needs and wasn't sufficiently attentive to the needs of the other person.

It may have been that I hurt someone by a cruel remark, a remark that came from my own need to put that person down in order to build myself up. In such a situation I was responding to a feeling of inadequacy and this dulled my sensitivity to the needs of the other. Or I may have hurt the other person by ignoring that individual or failing to work at maintaining the relationship. Such insensitive behavior on my part may not really reflect an absence of care for the other. It may have been more a matter of preoccupation with my own cares. I may have allowed myself to get so caught up with my own worries, hurts, or problems that I simply forgot about my friends and thereby hurt them.

But what about bigger hurts? Have I ever been responsible for hurting someone in a more major way—possibly through a failed marriage, a breach of a business contract, or even as the one who abused and violated the

rights of someone who was dependent on me or in some
way vulnerable? This sort of questioning will be very
difficult and we will probably require the help of someone else to answer the question. But if we do begin to
understand what was going on in us to allow us to
behave in such a hurtful manner, we will undoubtedly
discover that once again we were acting out of our own
needs, inadequacies, limitations, and brokenness.

While asking these sorts of questions takes real
courage, it can be unusually productive. The reward for
such self-examination is the ability to identify with
those who hurt us. Such identification breaks down the
artificial compartmentalization of the world into villains and victims. The reality is that we are all both villains and victims, and consequently none of us are simply one or the other. Both are caricatures. Even the most
evil person can be understood as acting out of his or her
own limitations and brokenness. And on this basis we
can identify to some extent with such behavior because
we see that we too hurt others for similar reasons.

I may have never hurt another by sexually abusing a
young child, or by destroying the character of someone
by means of slander and lies, or by violating a marriage
through adultery. But I am capable of any and all of
these acts. And until I can recognize that "there, but for
the grace of God, go I," I am incapable of experiencing
full and complete healing of the depths of my hurts.
When I can allow myself to identify with those who
hurt me by seeing myself to be made of the same basic
fabric, then, and only then, will I be able to understand
my reaction to them and fully release the anger. Only
then will forgiveness be something other than an act of
condescension which is never a satisfactory basis for a
genuine release of anger.

I am aware that my suggestion that we should be able

to identify with those who hurt us may strike you as strange. Particularly if you have been hurt by someone in a premeditated or repeated act of abuse, it may be difficult to see how identification with the one who hurt you is either desirable or possible. Let me explain this more fully.

According to Scripture, the primary source of temptation to do evil is not external but rather internal. The human heart is presented as deceitful and desperately wicked and as the source of the evil that we do (Jer. 17:9; James 1:14; Mark 7:21). In biblical psychology, the heart is the deep center of personality, the core of the human condition. Since the fall, we all inherit the same heart, that is, an essential rebellion against God which, left to run its own course, could lead any one of us to the most heinous of sins. This is a basic, even if tragic, part of the human situation. Our only hope of changing it is to first accept it as true. This fundamental insight is echoed in the words of Father Brown, G. K. Chesterton's fictional priest-detective, who reminds us that "no man's really any good until he knows how bad he is, or might be."

It is spiritual pride that makes us refuse to identify with another human, Christian or non-Christian, in their brokenness and sin. We want to distance ourselves from some kinds of sinners and in so doing we refuse to acknowledge the possibility of that same sin in ourselves. But if Christ could say that there was no temptation that he was not subject to, how can we afford to further distance ourselves from the temptation to sin than he did?

I well recall my own struggle on hearing of the arrest of a very good friend on charges of child pornography and pedophilia. This news came as a complete shock to all who knew this man, even to his wife and family. But what made this news most difficult for me was that my friend was both a Christian and a fellow mental health professional. Over and over again I asked myself (and him), "How could he have engaged in such behavior and at the same time maintained his other professional and religious activities and commitments?" This was really more an expression of my rage than of my intellectual questioning. How dare he present himself as a Christian and as a mental health professional while at the same time sexually abusing young boys and trafficking in child pornography!

While the strong feelings produced by this situation were not easily or quickly resolved, the turning point came when I was able to identify with my friend once again. He told me of his own abusive experiences as a child, something I knew nothing of before. He also told me the elaborate rationalizations he had developed over the years. They sounded rather weak to me but I began to recognize how weak mine would sound to others if they were similarly exposed. In short, I became aware that I too act out of my brokenness; that I too am a master of deceiving myself about my true needs and motivations; and that I too hurt others in ways I never intend as I live life out of my brokenness and sin. This does not condone my friend's behavior. He is currently in prison and this, even in his own assessment, is where he should be. But he is not really as different from me or you as the situation suggests.

Identifying with the one who hurts us is often exceptionally difficult. You should not feel guilty if you are unable to do so. I think that the eyes necessary to see ourselves and the one who hurt us in this new light are a special gift of God. I personally find that when I am ready to ask God to help me see the other person and myself as he does, that is, through his eyes, I am well on my way to being ready for healing. And God will assist us in developing this new perception, a perception of truth.

Seeing myself as more like than unlike the one who hurt me means that I am also one who needs forgiveness. Hopefully, in this realization I am also aware of having received such forgiveness from others in the past. As we will see in the next chapter, if I have never known the experience of forgiveness, it is extremely difficult (if not impossible) to give such forgiveness to someone else. But if, in seeing myself as one who has hurt others and who needs their forgiveness, I can then recall the experience of having been forgiven, I am then well on the way to being ready to give that forgiveness myself.

Summary

We have seen that the intellectual task of emotional healing involves reinterpreting the hurt which we experienced. This includes ensuring that my recall of the events of the hurtful transactions is as accurate as possible and, more importantly, allowing myself to identify with the one who hurt me. Identification requires that I correct my perception of both myself and of the other person, recognizing that we are more similar than dissimilar. This then prepares me to forgive while avoiding the trap of condescension.

The essence of this reinterpretation of my hurt is seeing those who hurt me as separate from what they did to me and seeing myself as more than my wound. When I see the other person as a person—broken, needy, and coping as best as possible with hurts and limitations—I begin to feel the first thawings of my hate. Hate becomes intermixed with compassion and this reflects the beginning movement toward the point where I can pray for them and wish them well.

When I see myself as more than my wounds—understanding that I too hurt others as I act out of my own brokenness, need, and woundedness—I am able to identify with the one who hurt me. This is something that I will initially resist. But it is essential. Hurts alienate and healing reconciles. The relationship with the one who hurt me is not always reconciled, but if I am to be healed of my wounds I must at least be reconciled within myself to the one who hurt me. This is the core of the hard work of forgiveness which will be our focus in the next chapter.

5

Releasing the Anger

The only remedy for the inevitability of our history is for-giveness.

—Hannah Arendt

True forgiveness is the hardest thing in the universe.

—David Augsburger

In the preceding chapter we saw that the process of healing emotional wounds necessarily involves not just the emotions but also the intellect. In this chapter, we come to the third component of personality involved in this process, the will. But we also come back full circle to the emotions because the volitional task in this third and final stage of healing is to release the anger associated with the hurt.

We mentioned in chapter 3 how easy it is to get stuck in feelings of anger. When we do, we sometimes erroneously assume that our stuckness means that more emotional work is still needed. Acting on such an assumption, we may continue to explore the feelings, trying to get to the bottom of our well of anger. But while being stuck in anger sometimes means that the core of the anger has not yet been reached, this is not always the case. As was noted earlier, exploration of feelings is necessary but not sufficient. A residue of anger may mean that more understanding is needed or that we now face the volitional challenge of releasing that anger.

Some people get stuck in their anger because they confuse expressing anger with releasing it. Expression of any feeling is almost always a necessary first step to releasing it, but expression and release are not the same thing. In expressing my anger I continue to embrace it. It is *my* anger, and for a while I may even feel glad that it is mine. It feels good to be angry. I am, at this stage, usually very aware that I am not giving it up, just expressing it.

As I am using the phrase, releasing the anger means giving it up. It means letting go of my right to revenge. It is forgiving other people for what they did to me. And this act of forgiveness, properly understood, is perhaps the most difficult thing a human being can ever be asked to do. Those who do not understand this have not yet faced a really significant hurt or have not yet attempted to let go of the anger associated with this hurt. To do so is to recognize that genuine forgiveness is never easy and that it usually involves the hard work of preparation, execution, and repetition.

Forgiveness: The Hard Work Miracle

While forgiveness involves great effort, these efforts do not produce forgiveness. Forgiveness is something that we do by a free act of our will, but the ability to forgive is a gift, even a miracle. This should not be understood as in any way minimizing the effort that is required. As stated earlier, no human action is more difficult than genuine forgiveness. However, the release of anger and the healing of damaged emotions that come from forgiveness is not something that I produce by my efforts. I do the hard work that is my part and then I receive the wonderful gift of forgiveness. It is something, therefore, that I should receive with gratitude.

Viewed in this way, forgiveness is like any of the other virtues. We love others, but can only do so by passing on to them something that is first given to us. It is the same with faith. Without faith, Scripture tells us that it is impossible to please God (Heb. 11:6). But while we are called upon to demonstrate faith, we must first receive it from God: "I do believe; help me overcome my unbelief" (Mark 9:24). It is the same with trust, hope, fidelity, and each of the other virtues.[1]

And so it is with forgiveness. We do our part and then we ask God to do his part. His part is in helping us release the anger and then in giving us the resulting emotional freedom and healing. I don't simply pray to God that he will render the other person forgiven by me. Unfortunately it is not that easy. I can and should pray that God would help me forgive the other person. This is a prayer he will answer because it is clearly something that he wills for me.

It is here that we need to note the relationship between receiving forgiveness and giving it. As it is hard to imagine how one could ever give love if he or she had never received love from another, so too it is hard to imagine how someone could forgive another if he or she had never received forgiveness. Knowing myself to be one who has needed and received forgiveness allows me to grant others this great and undeserved gift. And supremely, knowing myself to have needed and received the forgiveness of God allows me to become a forgiving person in a way that is quite impossible when only dealing with the experience of forgiveness as received from the hands of fellow humans. "God's forgiveness toward me and my forgiveness toward another are like the voice and the echo."[2] Without the former, the latter is both impossible and a meaningless absurdity.

This is the way in which forgiveness is a gift. I can give it because I have already received it. I didn't have to earn it from those who gave it to me and similarly, those who hurt me can do nothing to earn it from me. Forgiveness is always a gift of unearned extravagance and generosity.

The Importance of Forgiveness

In spite of the fact that the importance of forgiveness has not been widely noted by psychologists, the overriding emphasis it receives in Scripture makes it a most important concept in Christianity. Throughout both Old and New Testaments we are presented with the supreme value of divine forgiveness of our sins and are repeatedly enjoined to forgive others for their sins against us. Jesus linked these two expressions of forgiveness to each other by declaring that "if you forgive men when they sin against you, your heavenly Father will also forgive you. But if you do not forgive men their sins, your Father will not forgive your sins" (Matt. 6:14–15). It would be hard to imagine how Jesus could have given the importance of forgiveness any more emphasis than this.

The process of confession, repentance, and forgiveness is at the core of the Christian model of healing of our alienation from both God and each other. But forgiveness involves even more than the healing of our relationships. Scripture also presents evidence for a link between forgiveness and health. David spoke of his "bones wasted away" through his groaning until he finally confessed his sins and received God's forgiveness

(Ps. 32:3). Jesus also demonstrated the close connection between forgiveness and physical health in his cure of the paralytic who was healed as a result of Jesus forgiving his sins (Matt. 9:1–8).

This close connection between forgiveness and health has recently also been noted by medical researchers. Recent research has shown that people who have a tendency to hold resentment and a related inability to forgive others are much more likely to develop both cancer[3] and heart disease.[4] An even more direct risk to physical life has been noted by psychiatrist E. Mansell Pattison, who suggests that murder typifies the ultimate failure to forgive another and suicide the ultimate failure to forgive oneself.[5] A failure to forgive others, and the accompanying resentment and bitterness, has also been reported to be the leading cause of burnout.[6]

In light of the destructiveness of resentment and the healing nature of forgiveness, it is important that we forgive others for their offenses against us as quickly as possible. Resentment is a poison that destroys our body, soul, and spirit, and we should, therefore, strive to neutralize this poison with the antidote of forgiveness as soon as we are able.

The Problem of Premature Forgiveness

It is also important to be aware that premature attempts at forgiveness can actually impede healing. Understanding the forgiveness process and being sensitive to the steps that are involved in it are, therefore, crucial if we are to successfully forgive others for significant hurts received at their hands and to be healed of the wounds associated with these experiences.

People often try to forgive others before they know that for which they are forgiving. They usually have not yet really allowed themselves to feel the hurt and are using forgiveness as a way to defend against the pain. These ritualistic and premature acts of forgiveness are usually quite meaningless and seldom do more than support denial. The preparation necessary for genuine forgiveness includes the preceding two stages of reexperiencing the emotions and reinterpreting the hurt. There are no shortcuts to this process of preparation.

But, as noted earlier, forgiveness is seldom a one-time affair. Usually we need to do it over and over again. In the light of this you might wonder if premature forgiveness is really as dangerous as I suggest. Surely every little bit helps. Even if the work of forgiveness is not complete with one effort, perhaps we should start it as soon as possible and work away at it whenever we have the opportunity.

The problem with this approach is that premature attempts at forgiveness seriously obstruct the emotional and intellectual work of the earlier stages. If I believe I have already forgiven the other person, why should I explore the hurt and express the feelings? In fact, this is the most frequently encountered reason I hear for people not wanting to deal with these feelings. But the truth is that I cannot really forgive another until I know the feelings I am releasing. And by "know" I do not mean mere intellectual understanding. I also mean the experiential knowing that results from the work of the first two stages of emotional healing.

Pronouncements of forgiveness prior to my feeling the hurt or anger can be helpful first steps toward forgiveness if they are understood to be just that—first steps. Offering such forgiveness, I should be aware that I will almost inevitably later feel hurt and anger, and that these will give me further opportunities for repeated offerings of forgiveness. However, if I view my first effort at forgiveness as all that will be necessary, and if I expect that on this basis I should not feel any hurt or anger, then I am using forgiveness to defend against hurt in a way that impedes healing.

The Forgiveness Process

Forgiveness is the capstone to the healing process. Building on the emotional and intellectual work described respectively in chapters 3 and 4, we are finally ready to release the anger associated with our hurt. But how, exactly, do we do this?

There is no simple cookbook approach to forgiveness. There are, however, some steps which, if followed, increase the chances of success in forgiveness. I will describe four such steps—understanding why I resist forgiveness, clarifying my misunderstandings about the nature of forgiveness, limiting my expectations about what will result from forgiveness, and letting go of the anger.[7] The first three of these are actually preparation for forgiveness, not the act of forgiveness proper. The actual act of forgiveness is so disarmingly simple as to be almost anticlimactic. But simple should not be confused with easy, even if release of anger, once all the preparatory work is completed, is as uncomplicated as letting go.

Understanding Why I Resist Forgiveness

Seldom are we ready to release the anger of a significant hurt until we understand why everything within us resists such a step. Forgiveness is often quite impossible when I attempt it solely by means of willpower. Understanding why I resist forgiveness is the first step in the forgiveness process and is essential if my will is to be free to act. There are many reasons for my natural resistance to forgiveness and these must be acknowledged if they are to be eliminated.

One very frequent reason for resistance to forgiveness is that I may feel it is my right to hold a grudge. In the experience of hurt my rights were trampled. Now I am going to stand on my rights and it only seems fair to conclude that I have a right to be angry. But accepting anger as a natural response to hurt is not the same as accepting it as a right. Standing on my right to hold a grudge is standing on dangerous ground. It is running the risk of chronic bitterness.

Another reason for my resistance to forgiveness is often that I may not yet be ready to give up the sense of power I feel over the person who hurt me. This is best understood by recalling the powerlessness that I experienced in the first stages of hurt. At that point I felt weak, vulnerable, and helpless. But my anger has now restored a sense of power to me and I may be reluctant to give this up.

The power that can come from anger associated with an emotional wound is quite clear when we recall how commonly we speak of forgiveness in terms of letting the other person off the hook. Look closely at this image of the other person on a hook. It's an image of a meat packing plant with the person who hurt me impaled and suspended by a meat hook. I have the power to leave that individual in anguish or to let him or her off the hook. Can there be any doubt as to why I may then resist forgiveness? In such a situation, forgiveness involves giving up my power, power that I hold over the other person by virtue of my status as a victim.

A related source of resistance may be my reluctance to give up the feelings of moral superiority I now enjoy in relation to the person who hurt me. My wound may have been the occasion for the development of a victim role, and I may now be exploiting this role as I nurse a feeling of smug condescension based on moral superiority. Such feelings are also very difficult to relinquish.

Sometimes I resist forgiveness because I equate my withholding of forgiveness with the punishment of people who hurt me. It is quite clear to me that such people deserve to be punished for what they did to me. I was hurt by their actions and so it only seems fair that they should pay for this by being hurt or punished in some way. It may, in fact, be accurate to conclude that they should be punished. However, the fallacy in this line of reasoning is the assumption that I am the one to do this and that I do so by withholding forgiveness. Vengeance and ultimate justice belong to God. They are his responsibility. Furthermore, while withholding forgiveness does indeed inflict punishment, this punishment is inflicted not on the other person but on myself. I must, therefore, give up the idea that it is my responsibility to punish people who hurt me and that I do so by withholding my forgiveness of them.

Another reason why I may resist forgiveness is that I may feel I can only forgive other people if they request it. In such a view, it seems like throwing seed to the wind to disperse unsolicited forgiveness. I may feel that other people need to come groveling to me, expressing sorrow and regret for their actions, and offering restitution and promises that they will never hurt me again. But is this really necessary for forgiveness?

I do not believe that it is. If it were, we could never forgive a person who was dead, and we would be bound to the emotional consequences of hurt for the rest of our lives. But this is not the case. My forgiveness is not dependent on any response from other people.

A variant of this source of resistance is feeling that I can only forgive other people if they deserve it. This may take the form of not letting them off the hook until they have learned their lesson. Under the mantle of these apparently noble intentions I conclude that my withholding of forgiveness is in their best interests—not for their punishment, but for their learning. I may judge that if I forgive them they will not continue to reflect on their misdeeds. I, therefore, set up some hoops through which they must jump before I am willing to forgive them.

This way of viewing forgiveness reflects the same sort of moral superiority described earlier. In such a view, forgiveness must be earned. But in reality, forgiveness is always unmerited. If people can do something to earn my forgiveness, they don't need it. Forgiveness has its meaning in the grace of God. His forgiveness of us is always a gracious and extravagant response to us. There is nothing I can do to earn God's forgiveness and there is nothing another can do to earn mine. Freely we have received, freely we must give.

A final reason for my resistance to forgiveness is that it makes me vulnerable once again. In the experience of hurt I felt vulnerable, exposed, and raw. In such circumstances it is common to seek protection, either by means of retreat or aggression, and when I once again begin to experience some sense of safety I am very reluctant to leave it. Everything within me recoils from taking steps that will lead me toward further vulnerability.

This is quite understandable. In fact, it is the most realistic of the sources of resistance we have considered. Forgiveness does involve risk and risk involves vulnerability. The major risk of forgiveness is that of further hurt. It often hurts even more when I am hurt a second or third time by someone I have previously forgiven.

But while there are risks to forgiveness, there are also risks to withholding forgiveness. And these risks are even greater. The risk of being unforgiving is a life of chronic bitterness and hatred. We noted earlier that this is a terminal condition, one that involves the destruction of body, soul, and spirit. The chances of damage to ourselves from withholding forgiveness are extremely high and we must, therefore, be careful to never underestimate these risks. The chances of a subsequent hurt at the hands of the one who hurt me are not to be ignored but are usually lower than the chances of hurt to myself if I withhold forgiveness. On this basis I would suggest that forgiveness is always the better risk.

Clarifying Misunderstandings of Forgiveness

The second step in forgiving someone is to make sure that my understanding of forgiveness is accurate. Misunderstandings of forgiveness are common, probably due in part to the fact that the concept is such a popular one. However, if these misunderstandings guide our efforts at forgiveness, we will inevitably fail in our efforts and will bog down in the feelings of hurt and anger.

To forgive is not to forget.

For example, one very common misunderstanding of forgiveness assumes that it involves forgetting. But the adage "forgive and forget" is not only misleading in the suggested ease with which it characterizes the action involved, it is also seriously misleading as to the outcome.

To forget a hurt is to repress it. And, as we have already seen, this is not a part of genuine healing. Forgiveness does not eliminate memory. Acts which have been forgiven are still available for recall. However, over time they should have less and less emotional pain attached to them. The sting of the memory should lessen as I move through the forgiveness process. The goal is remembering without feeling malice. This is the sign that forgiveness has completed its healing work.

While I still should expect to be able to remember the hurt after forgiveness, I should also expect that I will be less and less preoccupied with it. In other words, forgiveness should afford me more control over memory. It should leave me free to recall the hurt if I choose but also free to not think about it once it comes into consciousness. Memory of the circumstances of the hurt will remain but should, over time, have less and less emotional energy attached to it. Only God can forgive and forget. The rest of us forgive and remember. But through forgiveness, we are able to remember without malice.

To forgive is not to excuse.

A second common misunderstanding of forgiveness assumes that it involves excusing the behavior of the one who hurt me. If I can excuse the behavior, forgiveness is unnecessary. But, on the other hand, it is precisely because the behavior of the one who hurt me is so inexcusable that I must forgive. Forgiveness is the only healing response to such injustice.

There are always reasons why other people behave as they do and sometimes these reasons will even make sense to us if we come to know them. However, reasons are not the same as excuses. There are reasons for everything we do in life, but some of what we do is still inexcusable. To make excuses for the other person is to engage in rationalization as a way of defending against the hurt. But in most instances of serious hurt, the behavior that hurt us is genuinely inexcusable.

Understanding the reasons why people who hurt me acted as they did can help me identify with them and, as we noted earlier, consideration of these reasons is part of reinterpreting the experience. This understanding does not, however, eliminate the hurt, hurt which can only be healed through forgiveness. Attempts to excuse will block efforts to genuinely forgive. Forgiveness must be given in the face of the inexcusable nature of the offense.

To forgive is not to ignore.

Attempts to ignore pain and hurt are sometimes also confused with forgiveness. In such situations I attempt to ignore the feelings of hurt, or even the person who hurt me. I simply try to get past the hurt by not thinking about it, by overlooking it in some way.

But this is also not forgiveness. Forgiveness does not involve overlooking the offense. It involves just the opposite. It involves facing it head-on. It requires thinking about the hurt and the one who hurt me. It involves accepting the experience as real, not attempting to minimize it. The hurt must be accepted as a part of reality. To ignore or to overlook it is an attempt to change reality by the power of selective attention. Such magical thinking does not produce genuine inner healing.

To forgive is not necessarily to extend unconditional trust.

A final misunderstanding of forgiveness involves the assumption that if I have forgiven people who hurt me, I should now be able to extend to them unconditional trust. Forgiveness, in such a view, is only complete if I can treat the other person as if the incident of hurt never happened.

This is really a variant on forgiveness as forgetting. It assumes that after the act of forgiveness I can act as if I don't remember what happened. This is impossible. We will remember and we must act in the light of that memory if we are to be responsible to ourselves and to the other person. Genuine forgiveness means that I no longer hold the hurt over the head of the other person. That is malice. It does not mean that I must assume that I will never again be hurt by them, nor does it mean that I should never take steps to minimize this possibility.

In some circumstances I may sense the other person's genuine remorse and conclude that I can safely extend complete trust without guarding myself further against recurring hurt. This assumption may turn out to be incorrect, but the choice is still usually the right one in the absence of a pattern of past behavior such as that which hurt me. It is better to occasionally be naive and be hurt a second time by someone than to be so untrusting as to never allow those who hurt me access to me again. However, in other situations caution and limited trust may be the most appropriate way of dealing with the person. Even so, my inability to extend unconditional trust does not mean that I have not genuinely forgiven the other person.

Think, for example, of a person who repeatedly steals things from you every time you invite him to your home. Or, an even more powerful illustration would be a babysitter who sexually abused your children while they were under her care. In such circumstances you would be called to forgive these people for these actions, but such forgiveness would not demand that you continue to offer them access to your home or to your children. In fact, we would probably conclude that anyone who did offer such continued opportunity was behaving irresponsibly. It is not being responsible to ourselves and our loved ones, nor is it being responsible to the person who continues to violate such trusts.

Similarly, people who repeatedly violate a trust of confidence should not be given further confidences. Or someone who repeatedly lies should not be given responsibility that would allow that lack of truthfulness to continue to hurt others. Forgiveness sometimes means that I will still have to be cautious around the one who hurt me. Unconditional trust is neither a necessary consequence nor an indication of forgiveness.

True Forgiveness

If true forgiveness is none of these things, what is it? Most simply, forgiveness is letting go of my malice and my right to retaliate and letting go of my right to hang on to the emotional consequences of the hurt. These are the things that I cling to as long as I refuse to forgive, and these are the things which in forgiveness I voluntarily choose to relinquish.

We should first note that no one can make us give up any of these things. In fact, as we know from experience, everything within us resists giving them up even when we choose to do so. To give these things up just seems to go against nature.

In some perverse way it seems that after being hurt I have a right to retaliation. I similarly feel a right to my anger, my hurt, and even to the self-pity that may accompany my perceived victimization. To give up these rights seems absurd, and to be asked to do so, quite unreasonable. But Scripture tells us that this is just what we need to do. God's Word to us always brings life and freedom and, although it may seem strange or even repulsive to us, his command to forgive others if we are to be forgiven by him is a brilliant stroke of healing grace. That which we most resist, giving up these perceived and perverse rights, is precisely what we need for our healing.

In forgiveness I give up the claim I feel I have on the one who hurt me. I consider the account to be balanced.

Anything I felt myself to be able to hold over the other person I now relinquish. Forgiveness is not repaying evil for evil or insult for insult, but giving a blessing instead (1 Pet. 3:9). It is wishing others well; it is praying that God will bless them and facing them in love, not hate. It is giving up my malice.

True forgiveness also involves relinquishing the emotional consequences of the hurt. I may continue to feel anger, hurt, depression, or other such consequences, but I choose to no longer embrace them. They are no longer my right. They are things that I now seek to leave behind me. Recurring waves of anger or pain remind me that healing is not yet complete, but they are not to be savored in self-pity. Rather, they are to be released as quickly as I am able to do so.

Limiting My Expectations
of What Will Result from Forgiveness

Before attempting to forgive the one who hurt me it is also important to have realistic expectations about what will result from the act of forgiveness. I have already indicated that the overall result of forgiveness should be that I am increasingly able to remember without malice. Let us examine this more closely to be sure that our expectations about what will result from the act of forgiveness are appropriate.

First, we should be clear about the fact that forgiveness may not heal the relationship with people who hurt us. They may not receive my forgiveness or may, in other ways, not be ready to change. My act of forgiveness should not be a gesture designed to manipulate them. Genuine forgiveness must be freely given. It can have no strings, conditions, or demands attached to it. It may be trampled or ignored, or it may be graciously received. I must give it without regard to these consequences. I give it because I choose to do so, not because of what it will lead someone else to do.

I recall a woman who worked with me in therapy for many months with the goal of forgiving her uncle for a series of experiences of childhood sexual abuse. During this time she never felt it necessary to communicate with him because she had neither seen him nor had any contact with him for over twenty years. However, after feeling herself to have successfully forgiven him, she decided that she wanted to communicate this fact to him. I urged her to be cautious in her expectations about how this would be received and tried to help her explore why she felt this action to be necessary. But her resolve to do so only strengthened, and so she finally wrote him a letter telling him she had come, over time and with difficulty, to forgive him for what he had done to her years earlier.

His response to this letter was immediate. He wrote back, denying the events to which she alluded, calling her (among other things) a liar, and threatening to sue her for slander and false accusations. She was absolutely devastated. All of her hard work in therapy seemed suddenly to be undone. Anger, depression, and waves of hurt and pain flooded over her once again. Forgiveness now seemed to have been a trap designed to further hurt her. The healing she had hoped and worked so hard for seemed illusory.

What this woman discovered as she worked through these feelings was that her forgiveness had been somewhat manipulative. She was hoping it would elicit an apology from her uncle, an acknowledgment that he was aware of how much she had hurt for so long, and some expression of sorrow for this fact. This was not to be, and she was making her healing dependent on his response. This was unnecessary. A gracious response on his part would have made it easier for her to totally release her anger, but she could deal with the hurt without his cooperation. She did not even need his acknowledgment that the abuse had occurred. She could forgive without any hope of a healing of the relationship.

This is what we see in Jesus' prayer of forgiveness from the cross. His plea to his Father to forgive those who crucified him because they did not know what they were doing expressed his own forgiveness of them as well as his realization that, in their ignorance, remorse was unrealistic. They were not about to feel sorry for that which they were doing, but this fact did not stop Jesus from forgiving them.

I must be guarded in my expectations and realize that forgiveness will most likely not automatically make me feel better. It is not a magic formula to eliminate pain. I must not doubt the genuineness of my act of forgiveness if I still hurt or feel anger after I forgive the person who hurt me. Over time I will begin to feel better, but this may not be (and in fact almost never is) immediate.

Finally, I must realize that forgiveness is seldom a one-time affair. Usually I must forgive over and over again. Each subsequent offering of forgiveness renders the former ones more complete. Each act of forgiveness is a giving up of all that I can give up at a particular time. Even so, with the passage of time I often better realize just how much there is that I am called to relinquish. Usually, therefore, I am called upon to forgive and to forgive again. With God, forgiveness is complete, and we need never ask again for his forgiveness for a previously confessed sin. But our forgiveness is seldom complete the first time.

Letting Go

I stated earlier that by the time we get to the actual act of forgiveness it may seem almost anticlimactic.

Forgiveness is, in essence, very simple. It is letting go—letting go of the anger, letting go of the right to retaliate, and letting go of the right to savor any of the emotional consequences of the hurt. But how do we do this?

I have already indicated that we should be prepared to do it slowly. We noted the dangers of premature forgiveness and my presentation of forgiveness as a process has repeatedly underlined the importance of patience in working through this process. But something needs to be added to this; it is also important to note that forgiveness should not be undertaken too slowly.

Earlier I described bitterness as a poison. Perhaps an even better metaphor is cancer. Nothing has the capacity to destroy us from within in quite the way hate does. The ancient Chinese proverb that "the one who pursues revenge should dig two graves" reminds us of the destructiveness of hatred and should alert us to the need to forgive as quickly as possible. Withholding forgiveness is embracing hatred and is, therefore, embracing our own destruction.

The advice to move toward forgiveness as quickly as possible is motivated by the recognition that if you wait for the circumstances to be just right, you will never forgive. If you wait until you feel like forgiving, you will never forgive. Or, if you wait until you have all the answers to your questions about your hurt, you will never forgive. Forgiveness is always offered in the midst of confusion and ambivalence. The best advice is not to loiter on your route to forgiveness. Make as much haste on this journey as is possible.

We should also make sure that we forgive specifically. Lewis Smedes says that only God forgives wholesale; we must be in the retail forgiveness business.[8] God can forgive us for all our sins, even apart from our enumeration of them. But we must forgive others for specific offenses, each specifically enumerated. Attempts at global forgiveness seldom have much meaning. This is the problem with premature forgiveness: we do not yet know that for which we need to forgive the other.

An aid to forgiving specific actions is to write down exactly what you need to forgive. This list should consist of behaviors, not personality traits. The focus of our forgiveness should be what other people did (verbs), not who they are (nouns and adjectives). We should not try to forgive someone for being obnoxious, selfish, or evil. Personality does not need forgiving; behaviors do. What we need to forgive others for are the specific things which they did that hurt us. And usually we are better able to do this if we first write them down.

Releasing the anger and renouncing the right to retaliate is often most meaningful when it involves some action or expression. This may, of course, be the action of going to people who hurt me and communicating to them that I have forgiven them for what they did to me. Or it could involve writing a letter to them communicating the same thing. But, in light of the earlier cautions about these direct expressions, other things are also possible and are actually often preferable.

One option is going through the written list and verbally expressing forgiveness for each specific item. After doing so, each should be crossed off and when completed, the list should be destroyed. I recall one man who attempted to follow this procedure but on completing the list decided to save it in case he ever wished to look at it again. He told me there was too much hurt involved in the actions he forgave to allow himself the risk of ever completely forgetting all the details. He was obviously not yet ready to forgive. He wasn't willing to let go of the hold he had over the one who hurt him, represented by his detailed documentation of the hurts.

Some people have reported finding great meaning in actually burning such a list, or in some other way physically destroying it. These rituals only serve to enhance the significance of the act of forgiveness. I once encouraged a couple to arrange some ceremonial way of observing their mutual forgiveness. Their response was a special dinner in front of their living room fireplace where they burned their respective lists of offenses and then went to church where their minister conducted a ceremony of recommitment to their marital vows.

The most important way in which we can seal an act of forgiveness is by wishing the other person well. If something direct is to be communicated to the one who hurt me, this is often the most important thing to communicate. I may do it in my behavior, showing friendliness and love rather than animosity. Or I may do it through prayers of blessing. Or I may do it through direct words. But it starts in my heart where I wish them well and I then look for ways in which I can communicate this new attitude of forgiveness to them. This is the seal on the act of forgiveness. As we noted earlier, forgiveness is giving a blessing rather than a curse, returning good for evil.

If you are unable to extend such a wish of well-being to the one who hurt you, you should not feel guilty. Guilt in such circumstances is counterproductive. Rather, do what you can do and pray that God will help you do more. Forgive as much as you can and be prepared to do so again in the future. But know that the process is not complete until the malice is gone and you are able to pray for the blessing of the one who hurt you.

Summary

We have seen that forgiveness is both difficult and yet simple. It is probably the hardest thing a human can ever be asked to do. But at the same time, once the necessary preparatory work is completed, it is quite simple. It is as uncomplicated as letting go.

Observing how young children forgive is often instructive in remembering just how simple the act of forgiveness is. It is sometimes quite disarming to be forgiven by a child. Such forgiveness is often so complete, so unqualified, so freely given. It is much more like the forgiveness of God than anything else we can experience. The forgiveness of a child can, therefore, teach us much if we are blessed by the opportunity of being forgiven by them for something we have done to hurt them.

This brings us back to the importance of our having experienced forgiveness if we are to communicate it to others. In fact, the quality of the forgiveness we have received from others will determine the quality of our own forgiveness. If all we have known is conditional and limited forgiveness, we will have difficulty extending more than this to others.

But complete and perfect forgiveness is available to all of us through God. My own offerings of forgiveness need not be limited by my past experiences of forgiveness. God's forgiveness of me can serve as both a model and as a source for my own forgiveness of others. I am not dependent on having had forgiving parents or experiences with young and forgiving children. A perfect heavenly Father stands ready and willing to forgive me each and every time I come to him requesting such forgiveness. And then, freely having received, I can more freely give.

Conclusion
Redemptive Possibilities in Suffering

One of the most troubling and difficult questions the thoughtful Christian can face relates to the presence of suffering in the world. Why is there so much suffering and pain? It doesn't seem fair that all of us have to suffer as much as we do and that some people's lives are so dominated by suffering. Where is God when we suffer? Where is he when young children are being sexually abused? How can he let such things happen?

There are no easy answers to any of these questions. Theologians and philosophers have struggled with them for centuries and are still far from agreement on an answer. Attempts to develop answers to such questions are described as theodicy, the justification of the ways of God to man. While there have been many such justifications, most of them are as unsatisfying as those offered by Job's friends in the face of his suffering.[1]

Some of the most helpful responses to the question of human suffering come not from theologians or philosophers but from ordinary men and women who have been extraordinary by their experiences of suffering. What these people offer us is not explanations of human suffering but ways of responding to it. And most impor-

tantly, many of them testify to the redemptive possibili-
ties that lie within suffering. What they suggest is that
of even more value than healing from our wounds and
relief from our suffering is meeting Christ in the midst
of our pain.

Sister Basilea Schlink, the founder of a Protestant
order of nuns, *Marienschwestern*, in West Germany,
attests to the unique opportunity to encounter Christ
and receive his love in our experiences of suffering. Her
advice is to say "Yes" to God in the midst of our suffering if we wish to receive his love and strength.[2] This
acceptance of suffering is neither a form of fatalism nor
is it mere resignation. It is an affirmation of the sovereign-
ty of a loving God who stands beside us as we face anything that he allows in our life. Edith Barfoot, who spent
seventy of her eighty-seven years in pain, also testifies
to the gracious presence of God she discovered in the
midst of her suffering. Deprived of movement, eyesight,
and hearing by advanced rheumatoid arthritis, she
affirmed suffering to be her calling in life, one in which
she claimed to discover meaning, purpose, and grace.[3]

Simone Weil also knew much pain in her short thirty-
four years of life, much of her suffering being voluntarily chosen as she identified with the poor, the disenfran-
chised, and the afflicted. During one experience of
intense suffering she described her encounter with God
as follows:

> Christ himself came down and took possession of me.
> . . . I had never foreseen the possibility of that, of real
> contact, person to person, here below, between a human
> being and God. . . . Moreover, in this sudden possession
> of me by Christ, neither my senses nor my imagination
> had any part; I only felt in the midst of my suffering the
> presence of a love.[4]

Experiences of emotional pain, as with suffering of any sort, can be unique opportunities to encounter God. This is not just a theoretical possibility. It is, as we have seen, the testimony of many people. Through suffering we are often able to discover God's presence, either for the first time, or, in some new and fresh ways. In *Traces of God in a Frequently Hostile World,* Diogenes Allen states:

> God is the ruler of all, so we can find his love even in and through our worst suffering. In all that is negative, something can be found that is positive and creative. . . . It is not by turning our backs on the harsh realities of life that we can find help in our daily lives, but by facing them, so that we do not merely keep our dreams of personal happiness alive but learn what happiness really is.[5]

A central thesis of this book has been the possibility of healing of our emotional wounds. Such healing means that we do not have to be victims of the hurts we receive but do not deserve. There is hope for healing of the tragedies and injustices of our life. This healing is always of God. It is never of our own making, nor is it produced by those who help us, either professionals or friends. They may be the agents of healing but its source is always God, whether we acknowledge him as this source or not.

But an even more important truth is presented to us in the reflections on suffering just noted. They suggest that we should not be content merely to seek healing of our afflictions. We should also seek God in the midst of our suffering. Viewed in this way, our hurts and the related suffering can often be a means of grace, a way in which God can uniquely touch us and give us the blessed experience of his presence. They can also be a means of growth for us if we do not simply get over the hurt and get back to where we were before, but rather expect God to use the hurtful experience to make us more whole and holy. Scripture speaks much of this redemptive function of suffering, and we are told that suffering can promote sanctification (1 Pet. 4:1–2), refine faith (1 Pet. 1:6–7), and build character (James 1:3–4).

Our hurts and afflictions can also give us something to offer to others. From experiences of hurt can come wonderful gifts of sensitivity to others who ache with hurt. This is one of the most beautiful ways in which God redeems our suffering. Out of the ashes of our affliction we often see God giving us something of great worth, something that we can pass on to others and that allows us to be of help to them when they suffer.

If the possibility of our healing is the good news of this book, the prospect of our meeting Christ in our suffering and of his using these experiences to make us more whole and holy is even better news. Jesus is indeed Lord of all and he seeks to meet us in every aspect of life, using each to further his work of our redemption. This is the best of all possible good news. It is the gospel.

Notes

Chapter 1

1. Frank Lake, *Clinical Theology: A Theological and Psychological Basis to Clinical Pastoral Care* (London: Darton, Longman and Todd, 1966). See also Frank Lake, *Tight Corners in Pastoral Counselling* (London: Darton, Longman and Todd, 1981).

2. Otto Rank, *The Trauma of Birth* (New York: Harcourt, Brace, 1929). See also Arthur Janov, *The Primal Scream* (New York: Putnam, 1970).

3. Statistics are drawn primarily from *Sexual Offenses Against Children* (vols. 1 and 2), a 1984 report of the minister of justice and the attorney general of Canada. This 1,300-page report was based on the examination of over 10,000 cases of childhood sexual abuse. Statistics for other Western countries are comparable. A good overview of what is currently known about the incidence, consequences, and treatment of sexual abuse is presented in Jeffrey Haugaard and N. Dickon Reppucci, *The Sexual Abuse of Children* (San Francisco: Jossey-Bass, 1988).

4. Judith Wallerstein, *Second Chances: Men, Women, and Children a Decade after Divorce* (New York: Tichnor and Fields, 1989). See also Judith Wallerstein and Joan Kelly, *Surviving the Breakup: How Children and Parents Cope with Divorce* (New York: Basic, 1980).

5. John Sanford, ed., *Fritz Kunkel: Selected Writings* (New York: Paulist, 1984).

6. I draw this notion of an implicit marital contract from Clifford Sager, *Marriage Contracts and Couple Therapy* (New York: Brunner/Mazel, 1976).

7. An excellent, although somewhat obtuse, discussion of these unconscious roots of our expectations of our spouse is presented by Henry Dicks, *Marital Tensions* (New York: Basic, 1967). See also

Victor Eisenstein, *Neurotic Interaction in Marriage* (New York: Basic, 1957).

8. Peter Bertocci, *Religion as Creative Insecurity* (Westport, Conn.: Greenwood, 1958).

Chapter 2

1. This framework for looking at life through the respective lenses of creation, the fall, and redemption is usually described as the Reformed perspective. An excellent presentation of that which is involved in making this a comprehensive Christian worldview is provided by Albert Wolters, *Creation Regained: Biblical Basics for a Reformational Worldview* (Grand Rapids: Eerdmans, 1985).

2. A computer search of over one thousand professional journals of psychology, psychiatry, and related fields identified only fifty-five articles in the last fifteen years that even mentioned the word "forgiveness." Of these, only a small handful provide a detailed consideration of the dynamics of forgiveness or its role in emotional healing.

3. There are a number of causes of depression and these often combine in any single depressive experience. Depression is a natural reaction to loss and this is probably the most common cause. (This is discussed more fully in chapter 3.) It can also apparently be produced by negative thoughts (although these are obviously sometimes a consequence rather than a cause of depression) and by a variety of physiological factors (including genetic, neuroendocrine, and neurotransmitter malfunctions). For a nontechnical overview of these and other causes of depression, as well as a helpful discussion of some practical ways of dealing with depression, see F. Minirth and P. Meier, *Happiness Is a Choice: A Manual of the Symptoms, Causes, and Cures of Depression* (Grand Rapids: Baker, 1988)

4. Bessel van der Kolk, ed., *Post-Traumatic Stress Disorder* (Washington, D.C.: American Psychiatric, 1984).

5. Ibid., p. 13.

6. The two major predisposing factors that are most usually hypothesized to be necessary for the development of multiple personality disorder are: (1) an inborn capacity to dissociate (usually best identified by a high degree of hypnotizability); and (2) repeated exposure to a traumatic and inconsistently stressful environment. For further discussion of the predisposing, precipitating, and perpetuating factors in multiple personalities, see Bennett Braun and Roberta Sachs, "The Development of Multiple Personality Disorder," in *Childhood Antecedents of Multiple Personality*, ed. R. Kluft (Washington, D.C.: American Psychiatric, 1985).

Chapter 3

1. This sort of simple cause-effect deterministic linkage represents a common but serious misunderstanding of Freud. In the first place, Freud was not as much of a determinist as he is usually represented to be and the sort of determinism that he built into psychoanalysis is not incompatible with a degree of human freedom and choice. The place of freedom in psychoanalytic psychology is well described in W. W. Meisner, *Psychoanalysis and Religious Experience* (New Haven: Yale University Press, 1984), pp. 205–18. Second, Freud repeatedly asserted that no single behavior or personality trait is caused by a single experience. What he called his principle of overdetermination noted that everything that is a part of our personality is there for multiple reasons (that is, it is overdetermined). Nothing is simply caused by some single experience.

2. Alfred Adler, *The Individual Psychology of Alfred Adler* (New York: Basic, 1956).

3. Sigmund Freud and Joseph Breuer, *Studies on Hysteria* (1895; reprint, New York: Basic, 1966).

4. For further discussion of the role of catharsis in psychotherapy, see M. Nicholds and M. Zax, *Catharsis in Psychotherapy* (New York: Gardner, 1977).

5. Sigmund Freud, "Mourning and Melancholia," in *Collected Papers*, vol. 4, ed. J. Riviere (1917; reprint, London: Hogarth, 1950).

6. Elizabeth Kübler-Ross, *On Death and Dying* (New York: Macmillan, 1969).

7. John Bowlby, *Attachment and Loss*, vols. 1 and 2 (New York: Basic, 1969, 1973).

8. C. S. Lewis, *A Grief Observed* (New York: Bantam, 1961), pp. 66–67.

9. I have developed this notion more fully in D. G. Benner, "The Incarnation as a Metaphor for Psychotherapy," *Journal of Psychology and Theology* 11(4): 287–94. Reprinted as *Therapeutic Love: An Incarnational Interpretation of Counselling* (Oxford: Clinical Theology Association, 1985).

10. See, for example, Jan Frank, *A Door of Hope* (San Bernardino: Here's Life, 1987). Although this book argues that direct confrontation of the person causing the hurt is always a necessary component of healing, in all other respects it is a helpful discussion of the route to emotional healing for victims of sexual abuse.

Chapter 4

1. William Glasser, *Reality Therapy* (New York: Harper and Row, 1965).

2. This definition of irrationality is adapted from M. C. Maultsby, *Help Yourself to Happiness Through Rational Self Counseling* (Boston: Malborough, 1975). Maultsby has been the major popularizer of the approach of Albert Ellis, whose ideas were most systematically presented in *Reason and Emotion in Psychotherapy* (New York: Lyle Stewart, 1962).

3. See Lawrence Crabb, *Effective Biblical Counseling* (Grand Rapids: Zondervan, 1977).

4. Adapted from T. J. Paolino, *Psychoanalytic Psychotherapy* (New York: Brunner/Mazel, 1981), p. 146.

5. Freud discussed the repetition compulsion often in his writings. A good overview is presented in his *Introductory Lectures on Psychoanalysis* (1917; reprint, New York: Norton, 1966), pp. 273–85. While he described the phenomenon quite accurately, he was not very successful in explaining it. Subsequent psychoanalytic theorists, particularly the British object relations theorists (see, for example, W. R. D. Fairbairn, *An Object Relations Theory of Personality* [New York: Basic, 1954]) have provided a better understanding, viewing the repetition compulsion as an attempt to solve old conflicts and trauma and thereby heal the ego splits that resulted from these unsatisfactory childhood relationships. The goal in psychotherapy guided by such an understanding is to replace repetition with remembering.

6. Lewis Smedes, *Forgive and Forget* (San Francisco: Harper and Row, 1984).

Chapter 5

1. See, for example, Erik Erikson, *Insight and Responsibility* (New York: Norton, 1964) for a discussion of the development of these and other virtues. In each case, Erikson argues that we must first experience the virtuous behavior in relationships with others before we can possess and demonstrate it ourselves.

2. Dennis and Matthew Linn, *Healing Life's Hurts: Healing Memories Through the Five Stages of Forgiveness* (New York: Paulist, 1979), p. 151.

3. S. Achterberg, S. Matthews, and O. C. Simonton, "Psychology of the Exceptional Cancer Patient," *Psychotherapy: Theory, Research, and Practice* 6(21): 13–14.

4. Redford Williams, *The Trusting Heart: Great News about Type A Behavior* (New York: Random House, 1989).

5. E. M. Pattison, "On the Failure to Forgive or to Be Forgiven," *American Journal of Psychotherapy* 31(1):106–15.

6. F. Minirth, D. Hawkins, P. Meier, and R. Flournoy, *How to Beat Burnout* (Chicago: Moody, 1986).

7. I am indebted to Lewis Smedes, *Forgive and Forget* (San Francisco: Harper and Row, 1984) for the framework and a number of the ideas in this discussion of the forgiveness process. I highly recommend his book for additional reading on the topic.

8. Smedes, *Forgive and Forget*, p. 147.

Conclusion

1. Although the theodicy of Job's friends is ultimately inadequate, the Book of Job is an invaluable study on the meaning of suffering. Other helpful biblical studies on the topic are found in 1 Peter, James 1, and Romans 5.

2. Basilea Schlink, *The Blessing of Illness* (Carol Stream, Ill.: Creation House, 1977).

3. Edith Barfoot, *The Witness of Edith Barfoot* (Oxford: Basil Blackwell, 1977).

4. Simone Weil, *Waiting on God* (Glasgow: Collins, 1959), pp. 35–36.

5. Diogenes Allen, *The Traces of God in a Frequently Hostile World* (Cambridge, Mass.: Cowely, 1981), p. 2.